20 Years in Tuscany

Adventures encountered during the
renovation of an ancient farmhouse in Italy

by Gillian Drake

SHANK PAINTER PUBLISHING

"You may have the world if I may have Italy."
— Giuseppe Verdi

ISBN: 978-1-888959-48-2

SHANK PAINTER PUBLISHING
P. O. Box 720, North Eastham, MA 02651

PRINTED IN USA

The Seed of an Idea

SOMETIMES it's difficult to remember how the seed for an idea that manifests itself decades later was first planted. When I think about it, it was on my honeymoon in 1969. We were both 21, and after a society wedding in a picture-perfect country church near Oxford, with a garden-party reception and guests arriving in top hats and Rolls Royces, we set off on our honeymoon in our British racing green MG sports car. With the top off, we sped along country roads from London to Paris and then to Fano on the Adriatic coast of Italy, and then on to Rome.

I think everyone assumed I was <u>that</u> kind of person, myself included—you know, with the handsome upper-crust boyfriend, an open-topped sports car, and a fancy wedding. In fact, I wasn't that kind of person at all, but it took me a few years before I found that out. For now, we were managing to live a good life, in those exciting "swinging Sixties" days, on very little income; he was an art dealer and I was a small-time antiques dealer with a stall at the Chelsea Antiques Market. We were just starting out, but the politics of the day seemed stacked against us; it was the time of student riots and coal-miners' strikes, of four-day weeks, bombings in Northern Ireland (especially painful for me as my father was Director of Ordnance Services for the British army and in charge of bomb disposal), and currency controls. We were only able to take 50 pounds each out of the country per year, carefully marked by fountain pen in the back of our passports by the local Post Office. That meant we had to manage a three-week vacation on 100 pounds; no wonder we ran out of money on the way back from Rome and had to spend the night in a field in Switzerland, sleeping in the car and being awakened at the crack of dawn by a flock of sheep surrounding the car with their bells clanging. But the breakfast we scrounged from the local farmer's wife, sitting outside her farmhouse drinking cafe au lait and eating freshly baked bread and homemade unsalted butter as the new day spread its gentle light on the mountain meadows, was one of the most memorable moments of our trip.

But the real coup de grace happened in Fano. I'd been there before with my family and we'd been introduced to a local character, Major Tom Storer. He had been in the British army, in the Sappers (Engineers), as they marched up the length of Italy, liberating the country from Hitler's grip, and after the battle of Monte Cassino had been billeted in the coastal fishing village of Fano. Here he met the local contessa—and married her. She was well padded financially and he'd lived a bucolic life ever since. But she was evidently tiring of him and his ways, and he was fast approaching the end of his cushy life of luxury. He'd decided he was a painter and he became a familiar sight all over town, painting rather dreadful views of the ancient Roman town and the beautiful lido on small canvases which tourists bought right off his easel. He introduced us to many of the local people and showed us the local haunts, so when I returned with my new husband on our honeymoon I looked him up and rejoined the local social scene. But the most memorable thing is that one day he took us up to an old farm overlooking the bay and showed us around. It was enchanting, with terraces of old gnarled vines reaching down to the glistening bay below. "It's abandoned," he said, "Why don't you buy it? It's only 500 pounds." It's all we talked about on the long trip back but we were just starting out and we simply didn't have the money, or any hope of raising it. So the dream drifted off into the far reaches of my mind and my life took me in very different direction from what I'd imagined, to America and a life in another fishing village, but this one at the tip of Cape Cod.

Italy had Touched my Heart

I HAD NEVER WANTED to rebuild a ruin. It wasn't a pressing dream of mine, like it is with some people. But I did want an old house. In Italy. It was a dream I'd had since I was 21, when honeymooning in Fano on the Adriatic coast of Italy. So it wasn't a dream that I'd read about, or seen in a movie, it was a dream based on reality, so close I could taste it. But we were young, just starting out, and by the time five years had passed, we had separated and I had started a new life in the US, pursuing a different kind of dream—the American Dream.

What they don't tell you about the American Dream is that fortunes can be lost as easily as they can be made, and I was at the lost-the-fortune stage when I met Ron in 1998 and in the process of getting my life back together and raising my daughter, then 14. He was an adventurer and ran safaris from London to Cape Town. After a series of marriages to rather dull men, this sounded like my kind of guy. And within a matter of months, I had sold a pair of diamond earrings to pay for a ticket to Nairobi and was off on my own adventure.

But Italy was always in the back of my mind. It had always felt like home to me, but with that frisson of mystique that makes something irresistible. I'd first gone there with my parents in the late 1960s, driving from England across France and Switzerland for a three-week family summer vacation. My father, being a very precise man, had figured out that if we caught the night ferry and then drove all day, we'd arrive in Switzerland by night fall and could reach the Adriatic coast by the end of the second day. That meant we would spend only one night, instead of two, in a hotel on the way. It was an exhausting trip, but full of romance and excitement, from the moment we

stepped foot on the cross-Channel ferry, manned by French sailors in
their matelot shirts, and crossed the English Channel at night, with
the black sea heaving around us and lights twinkling in the darkness. Then the unfolding of the maps—no GPS in those days—and
marking off the French towns: Amiens, Soissons, Chalons. And on
to the border crossing into Switzerland, the showing and stamping of
the passports, the climb up the mountain pass to the snow line, the
descent down to the lakes gleaming in the sunshine, and at last our
Swiss chalet and a bed for the night. Then the early morning start
after a café au lait and a croissant and the tunnel into Italy, arriving in
the Val D'Aosta, an impossibly beautiful place, so much more foreign
seeming than domesticated France, with its bourgeois manners and
focus on appearances—here the focus was on living. And living with
gusto. There was a different kind of energy, different smells, different
colors. And the landscape was breathtaking. I'd never seen anything
so beautiful as Lake Como. The autostrada system had just been
built, so after we reached Milan we were on main roads all the way
to the east coast. And then to arrive at the fishing village of Fano, to
find our apartment on a cobbled street overlooking the port and the
hustle and bustle of the fishing boats, to stroll along the quay and see
the restaurants grilling squid and fresh sardines on charcoal grills,
and the beautiful sweep of the bay, golden sand against turquoise
seas under an azure sky. The old Roman town center, the daily street
market, the wine merchant making his daily rounds with a huge vat
of wine on a cart pulled by a grey donkey, bring out your bottle and
fill it up from the spigot—it was enchanting, it was seductive, it was
life changing.

I remember exactly the moment I felt I could live in Italy. In those
days, people danced. There were dances everywhere, organized by
everyone from the local tourist board to individual restaurants. My
brother and I had fallen in with a bunch of Italian teenagers and
had been swept up in their lives, racing in old cars from a football
match to a pizza joint and even one trip to a night club on the other

coast of Italy and babbling away in a mix of languages. In those days, our French was much better than our Italian, but we all managed to understand each other. One of these was a young student called Maurizio. He was a bit of a playboy, hitting on the English tourists who visited the town each summer. I had a boyfriend back home, but was not immune to the charms of a potential Latin lover. I remember dancing with him at an open air dance by the bay, swirling around in his arms with the mountains a ring of fairy lights around me, fire-flies in the background, and he kissed me as only a Latin lover can, and me thinking to myself, Yes, I could live here. Of course, nothing came of it; I packed up my pink gingham bikini and chic matching head scarf and headed back home to the grey UK with my family a few days later and forgot all about him. Or did I? I found out on another visit to Fano a few years later than he'd continued to play the field, but had had to get married to a young Italian woman he'd got pregnant—apparently he was playing a kind of Russian roulette.

So the seeds were well sown for my Italian dream, all that was required was the opportunity. But Cape Cod was a long way from the Mediterranean, and opportunity seemed like a remote idea.

But opportunity did finally come, strangely enough, because of two tragic events. The first was that my cousin, an Olympic sailor, was swept overboard and drowned while skippering the sail boat called the Sword of Orion in the Sydney to Hobart race on the day after Christmas in 1999. The second was the attack on the World Trade Center in the US on September 11th, 2001. We had planned to take a group of guests on a special bird-watching safari to Tanzania in October of that year, but after the 9/11 tragedy, we cancelled the trip. Instead, we decided to go to Italy—it seemed closer to home, less foreign, somehow, and it was more than 30 years since I had last visited the country. Ron had an uncle, born in Italy, who had recently returned to live in Milan with his sister after his wife had passed away, so we used them as our base and traveled around from there.

We rented a car and drove to Asti, where we drank Barolo wine and ate truffles, visited the Ligurian Riviera, stayed in an old palazzo in Siena, and saw so many Italian hill towns we couldn't tell them apart any more. We arrived in Assisi in a drenching downpour and stood in line to see the remarkable *chiesa* of Saint Francis, and then headed up the coast towards Venice and spent four or five days in La Serenissima, freezing our butts off (it was November) but loving every minute of it. But when we returned to Milan, I realized that there had been little evidence of the Italy I'd fallen in love with more than 30 years earlier. It was a great trip, but it lacked a certain something—that true Italian flavor. That's the trouble with the tourist route, you don't get to see, to experience, to feel, the real Italy. And I remembered what it was like back then, and I wanted to re-experience that again. Either it didn't exist any more, or it had eluded me.

Soon after, we visited the UK and saw my cousin Merrion, whose brother had drowned in the sailing accident. She told me that she had bought an old ruin in a remote part of northern Tuscany with the proceeds from his estate, and was going to call it Casa Glyn, after his name, Glyn Charles. When I heard this, the words just came out of my mouth: When my father dies, I'm going to buy a house in Italy. Where did that come from, I thought? But after it had sunk in that I'd actually voiced that long-time dream out loud, I realized we didn't have to wait—we could do it now. Let's look for a house!

The next September, we went to stay at Casa Glyn, even though the renovations weren't finished, as Ron, who is a brilliant handyman, had told Merrion that he would do some electrical work in return for us staying there. We flew to Milan (in those days you could fly direct to Milan from Boston via Alitalia), visited Ron's uncle Petronio, and rented a car and drove to Lunigiana, in northern Tuscany, so-called by the Romans as the region seemed to them to resemble the mountains of the moon. We took Petronio with us. We stopped for lunch in Aulla, since it was a Sunday—Petronio was Italian and it was part of his tradition—and had a wonderful meal of sizzling grilled local meats, the specialty of the house. Then we headed up the mountain above Fivizzano to the little village of Cotto and after losing our way a couple of times and getting stuck in some very narrow lanes, nearly burning out the clutch of our rental car as we backed out, we arrived at last and were greeted by Merrion's neighbor Ava, who was holding a rabbit by the ears, obviously her dinner. Yes! I thought; this is my kind of place! The view of the Apuan alps (the marble mountains of Carrara) in the distance was spectacular. I felt I had re-discovered the real Italy—off the beaten tourist-track where almost no one spoke English, the shops closed for two or three hours at lunch time, and you could get a three-course meal for 10 euros including wine. Yes! This was it, a beautiful place where you could still find a ruin to fix up for a reasonable price, and what an adventure that would be!

Merrion's neighbor Ava, Peter and Gillian at the moment we first arrived in Cotto

Finding the House

BOTH RON AND I tend to get easily bored on vacation. We are "doers"—we need to have something to do, to work towards, something that gives us a sense of purpose and builds value. Rather than go on a two-week vacation to an exotic location, we wanted to have more—to learn a foreign language, to get to know the local people, to be part of a culture that was new to us. And we realized if we wanted to do that, we would need to have a house to look after with some land to keep us busy. We had traveled extensively in East Africa and had seen how our friends lived there, both in Nairobi (Kenya) and Dar es Salaam (Tanzania), with *askari*—guards—protecting their property 24 hours a day and a series of walls surrounding their house, plus a strong room inside the house where things of value were stored, a room with no windows and a heavily protected locking system that you had to put your hand up into it so no thief could pick the lock. And although property was affordable—even beach front property—we didn't want to live that way. Our friend Gary, who had a house on the beach in a suburb of Dar es Salaam, found he wasn't able to protect his house from thieves on the exposed beach front and was robbed a few times. And other friends, who were part-owners of a family property in Algiers, Morocco, had installed a married couple as caretakers to live in a part of the house full time, but they turned out to be corrupt and they stole everything, including the car from the garage and the bathroom sinks off the wall.

So we decided that Italy was the perfect place—we loved the food, the history, the language, the people—and the wine! And it was safe, in a first-world country. We reckoned we could afford a little house for about 50,000 euros; it would give us a foot-hold in Europe, and since I was born in Wales and most of my family lived in the UK, I would be heading east to visit them anyway and we would just keep on heading in that direction.

While we were staying at Casa Glyn, we had met Simon Foster, the Englishman who had overseen the renovations of my cousin's house. We mentioned we might be interested in looking at some houses that were suitable for renovation so we agreed to meet him and his realtor friend Federico Cardalini in Pontremoli (the capital of Lunigiana) the next day. It turned out to be a miserable rainy day but we decided to go ahead with the day's plans anyway. When we met up with them, they had a binder of faded Polaroid photos for us to look through, which ranged from the unappetizing to the downright dismal. But I spotted one that looked like it had potential—I saw two stone gateposts opening onto a stone-flagged courtyard, albeit overgrown with weeds, which spoke of a dignified past.

Ron and Gillian in front of the ruined house on the day they first saw it

It turned out that Simon had not seen this particular house before, otherwise he might have snapped it up and marketed it to some British or Americans as a renovation project. As he had business to attend to elsewhere, we drove with Federico over the mountains to a valley to the south of Fivizzano and to the small village of Reusa in the commune of Casola. When we had seen the photo of the house, we assumed it was only one floor, but we discovered, on actually seeing it in person, that there were two more levels beneath the top floor, going down the hillside. The top floor was living space, but the two lower floors had been used for animals—cattle, chickens and rabbits—and it smelled like it. In all, we counted at least a dozen rooms, including an illegally built (*abusivo*) kitchen which had been built over the Roman road that ran below it, completely obscuring the view. We had to remove that room—the laws of Tuscany decreed it; we would lose a room but it would reveal the view in all its glory. We explored the rambling old (and ruined) house and then, fearing

View of the old kitchen that had been built illegally and was obscuring the view of the mountains; this photo was taken the day we first went to see the house and the bad weather meant we could not see the mountains so we did not realize there was a magnificent view!

we were about to do something totally crazy, drove to the coastal town of Lerici to stay overnight and try to come to our senses. We made a list of pros and cons and to our surprise the pros far outweighed the cons. A great view: check. On the edge of a small village: check. An historic house with great "bones": check. Surrounded by beautiful scenery: check. Nosey neighbors: check (so we wouldn't be burgled while we were away). We decided that we should go ahead and buy it, but agreed between us that we understood that the project would most probably cost twice as much and take twice as long to complete than we anticipated.

The view of the mountains from one of the terraces

We had seen the house in a chilly September drizzle, so opaque we didn't even realize there was a view of the mountains, but when we went back the next day to take a second look at "our" house and saw the village bathed in golden autumn sunlight, with the Apuan Alps shimmering against a cerulean sky, the house seemed to speak to us; "Save me, buy me, love me" it said. It was hard to resist, because it felt like the right thing to do. By then we were hooked—on the magnificent view, the charm of the village, the valley it overlooked, and the historic quality of the old house—and there was no turning back.

It was beyond our budget, but look at what we were getting! We were completely sold; it was to be our house, our newest project, a new direction in life.

The side of the villa as it looked on the day we first saw it

Nuts and Bolts

WHEN WE CAME BACK to the US and told our friends that we had bought an old ruin in Italy, they asked us, What's the plan? And we would say, There is no plan—we are just going to take it one day at a time and renovate the property and see where that leads us.

The house was actually two pieces of property—the large house plus a little terraced house attached to it to the north and an adjacent barn, actually a chestnut-drying house. But we weren't buying all of the little terraced house, just half of the upstairs and a quarter of the downstairs, which would be our wine cellar. It Italy, it is common practice for a property to be divided up amongst all the children when a parent dies, sometimes leaving an inheritance of no more than one room—so different from the British system of leaving everything to the oldest son so the property is kept intact.

For those who are interested, or think they would like to do something similar, I'm going to talk about money. The house was listed for around 60,000 euros, and the attached terraced house and small barn added another 12,000 euros to the price, for a total of 72,000 euros. To purchase the property, we mortgaged Ron's family home in the historic South End district of Boston, which after the exchange rate and professional fees amounted to $100,000.

We applied to our local bank in Italy for a mortgage and, amazingly, the bank offered to lend us 190,000 euros—which seemed like a huge sum—to renovate just the top floor. That was back in the heady days of 2002, when the euro was new and on par with the US dollar and everyone was dizzy with the idea of easy money—so different from today. But after a year, we realized that to pay back the mortgage on the property we'd need to rent it out as a luxury villa. And to do that, we needed to install a swimming pool. On our hillside of rubble. And so began the process of building a series of retaining walls. They cost 10,000 euros a wall, and we needed six walls—plus the cost of building the pool, which was about 25,000 euros.

After our neighbor Roberto died, we purchased his barn and a piece of land for the swimming pool from his widow Lina and her two sons; we had to do this as the laws of Tuscany decreed that we had to build the swimming pool further down the hillside from the church, as it was a Grade A listed building. It was when Massimo was excavating the wall of the terrace that we'd purchased from our neighbors and he was too enthusiastic with his digger that the wall collapsed. Fortunately no one was hurt. That was when we found out that when we bought the terrace, we had also bought the wall. So we had to spend another 10,000 euros to rebuild the wall and face it with stone. That is the law in Tuscany—any retaining wall that is built in an historic district has to be designed by a licensed engineer, reinforced with steel and concrete, and faced with stone, so it looks like an old wall.

The house was a disaster zone, with a leaking roof and rotting beams and rain-soaked plaster. Simon found a crew that would take on this project and they cheerfully started work. They removed the roof and the floors/ceilings and the windows and doors so that all that was left were the stone walls—you could look down from the top and see clear down to the basement. We salvaged every single thing we could from the wreck of the original building: beams that weren't sodden, terra cotta floor tiles from two bedrooms which we relaid in the dining room and kitchen, and usable planks from the floors which we had milled to go in the cathedral ceiling of the living room. Looking back, I can't believe that we were foolish enough to buy such a run-down place, nor that we had found a building company that was willing to take on such as project. It was like having a boat—as the saying goes, it's like pouring money into a hole in the ocean. But we were lucky, we had found a crew whose motto was "nothing is impossible" and we were able to raise just enough money, over the years, to finish the job.

My bible for the renovation was a coffee-table book, lavishly filled with mouth-watering color photos, entitled "Renovating a House in Italy" by Elizabeth Helman Minchilli. Not only was it filled with quite lovely photos of different styles of renovated villas from every part of Italy, but it had some very useful information about mundane things like roof beams, tiling, and wall plaster. One thing I learned from the book was to use tinted plaster on the walls, rather than white plaster that was then painted, and to apply it by hand so that it shimmered like silk.

When the renovations were finished, the property consisted of a five-bedroom/five bathroom villa, with the converted chestnut-drying house providing a sixth bedroom/bathroom, plus a large two-story barn, another chestnut-drying house, which we decided not to convert as we preferred to leave it as a kind of museum, and three acres of land that included terraced gardens, an olive grove, and a swimming pool—plus some pieces of land that we never found. In the end, it turned out that not only did it not cost twice the estimate to renovate it, but more like five times! So we had no option but to rent it out for the summers. And so began our adventures as villa owners, with Ron acting as handyman, pool guy and housekeeper, and me as booking agent, website designer, interior designer, and gardener.

The following essays and notes are ones I wrote over the 20 years that we were owners of this property. I hadn't planned on making it available as a book, but several of the people who read it thought I should do it. And so I have! They are mostly arranged in chronological order, and I hope they convey to you some of the excitement and enthusiasm we had for this project, and also of our love for Italy and her people.

Our Neighbor Roberto Tonelli

October 2005

I WAS THINKING OF THE adventures I've had in the last seven years since I met Ron—traveling the world, fixing up houses, and having enough money not to have to worry about it. It's been great. But fixing up this house in Italy is the best adventure yet. It really is the thrill of a lifetime, to find a decrepit old ruin of historic value and bring it back to life, to create something beautiful out of a crumbling shell of stone and terra cotta tiles that the villagers had given up for lost. And I got to thinking about our beloved neighbor Roberto, such a special soul. I remember when we first saw him—it was the second visit we made to the house, well, let's be honest and call it a ruin, a *rustico*.

He was sweeping sawdust and fallen leaves into a small pile to make a bonfire. I remember feeling so happy because I thought that he was all of 65, and would be around for a long time, so would be able to initiate us into the mysteries of Italian country ways, such as making olive oil and homemade wine. I was shocked to find out a little while later that he would turn 80 that November. And just a year later he would be dead. But in that time, we forged a firm friendship.

He had been born in America, his father having emigrated there early in the 20th century. But when the depression made life too difficult in America, his father returned to the family's house in Reusa with his youngest son to eke out a living from the land, leaving his other three sons in America. Roberto met his future wife, Lina, who was born in the tiny neighboring village of Groppolo, and married her and they had lived that way ever since, planting and pruning according to the phases of the moon, tending a few cows, keeping chickens, bottling tomatoes and preserves, and making olive oil and wine to last them throughout the year. I was content to know that we could, with their tutelage, become part of the old Italian way of living off the land, even if only for a few months a year.

But when Roberto died in the spring of 2004, just a few months after my own father's demise, it signaled to me the gradual fading away of this so-called "greatest generation," with their heroism and war stories. It seemed like the end of an era, and the end of a way of Italian country life that had been continuous for centuries, but would be no more. And we had just missed out on it. I enviously heard our neighbors Anne and Geoff, a British couple who had moved to the neighboring village of Vedriano some twenty years earlier, tell of village picnics in the mountains, of porcini hunts and riotous outdoor parties with music and homemade food and wine, and it saddened me to realize that the old way of country life in Italy was fading away, just as the entire generation was.

Gillian with neighbors Lina and Roberto Tonelli in the courtyard of their historic old house in Reusa, September 2003

And now we watch as Maurizio, Roberto's younger son, working three jobs to support his wife and two sons in their newly-built house in Casola (his wife did not want to move into the ancient family house in Reusa, like most Italians she wanted something more modern that would not remind them of their impoverished past), and in the evenings helping his mother with the *vendemmia* or the olive harvest or setting smoky fires to keep the wild boar out of the olive groves, where they grub under the olive trees, uprooting the grass. But maybe when Maurizio retires from his municipal job at the *comune* (town hall) in Casola he may come to live in Reusa and take up the life his father led. But if he does he will be in the minority. And so these little hill towns and villages are falling into decay and the ancient stone houses are being bought up by the British and the Germans—and yes, the Americans—and turned into holiday homes and bed and breakfasts, or snapped up by couples from Milan looking for an inexpensive country escape. Are we part of the problem, I wonder? And then I think, well if not for us, it would be someone else renovating our house . . . and I remember that when the village priest along with the villagers decided that they wanted us to buy the ruined *canonica*, the old priest's house that sits in our olive grove, becoming more ruined every year after it was pretty much destroyed in an earthquake in the 1920s, they explained to us that they "didn't want Germans to buy it because they'd be drinking beer and jumping into a swimming pool"—right next to the church. Memories are long and feelings from the war still run deep; there is a shrine just up the road, which the villagers still decorate with flowers, that marks the spot where a young lad had been sitting by the roadside during the war when a couple of passing Nazi soldiers had lobbed a hand grenade at him for no apparent reason, blowing him to smithereens.

A Day in the Life, Italian-Style

c. 2005

WE HAVE JUST RETURNED from lunch with our crew—Angelo, the boss, his father Delio, his partner Stefano, and workers Riccardo and Ucho—at the new *agriturismo* which has, *grazie a dio*!, recently opened just down the road from our tiny village—a 10 minute walk down the hill, though a 20 minute walk back up. The food is superb. As an *agriturismo*, in exchange for a construction grant from the government, the new inn has to serve at least 50 percent of its food from its own land, so the olive oil and wine come from the inn's olive groves and vineyards, fresh vegetables are from its farm, and the pasta and desserts are home-made. For lunch, we consumed three bottles of red wine with a three-course meal, for 10 euro each, before

Spino Fiorito when it first opened

returning to work at two, the guys having left work at the sound of the church bell at *mezzogiorno e mezzo*, 12:30 (twelve bongs and a clank, from the cracked half-hour bell). Today we were served a robust *minestrone*, followed by a choice of eggplant parmigiana (not breaded as in the US), *salsicce* (sausages) with stuffed cabbage, or *arrosto imbottito* (stuffed roast beef.) Everything was quite delectable. The meal, at which we rattled away in broken Italian, getting more fluent with each glass of wine, was excellent, and was followed by homemade blackberry tart, espresso coffee, and a special liqueur of the house, flavored by some herb that autumn sunlight and agreed that this is *il melio luogo nel mondo*, the best place in the world! Riccardo disagreed, he has been to India, but the rest of us were in accord.

As I write this, Ron and Stefano interrupt me brandishing the first bottle of this season's wine from our neighbor's cantina, whose grapes we helped pick just ten days ago. This is not as good a season as last year, too much rain in August, but by *gennaio*, January, they say, this new wine will be good to drink. But it's quite drinkable now, at less than two weeks old. With no additives, no sulfites, and no added sugar or yeast, we have found that we can quite happily drink half a liter for lunch and return to work with a warm glow but no greater after-effects, a custom our crew follows daily, though I do remember Angelo nearly falling through the roof after one particularly extravagant lunch a year ago or so.

This morning before lunch we took a trip to Fivizzano, a picturesque market town in another valley about 15 minutes north of Reusa, to do our shopping in the weekly outdoor market. There we met my cousin Margaret (the widow of my mother's first cousin David, and mother of Merrion and Glyn) for a cappuccino in the town square. There are three cafes in the ancient piazza, and one chooses where to sit depending on whether it's morning or afternoon, and whether one desires sun or shade. This morning we chose the sun, reveling in the glorious autumn weather, and were served by one of the identical twins who run this particular *gelateria/café*. At first we were baffled by being served our coffee by one women and then being asked about what we had ordered so she could prepare a bill by seemingly the same woman. It took a while to realize they were *gemelle*, twins, which I'm sure has caused many similar confusions. Interestingly, as they age, they become less identical, one being better looking than the other.

The market is lively today, everyone is out enjoying the weather—after all, it may be the last warm, sunny day, who knows? We have had an amazing spell of summery weather this October, and each day seems to show more defiance of the winter that we know must follow. I circle the market stalls and buy a plump buttery lettuce and a huge yellow pepper for 90 centimes, about a dollar ten, and then queue up at the fish truck for a much anticipated treat, fresh fish! This week I opt for two fresh sole, which the fishmonger strips of innards and skin while I wait. The cost is dear, ten euros for two little fish, bones in, but fresh fish is hard to come by in this inland region, though at only 30 miles from the Mediterranean, it would appear by other standards, Kansas, for instance, that we are virtually on the coast.

Every area in Italy is devoted to its *casalinga*, its own style of food, and in this area, the Lunigiana, locally-raised meat, pecorino cheese from mountain sheep, and local specialties such as spinach pie, pesto, and walnut sauce for pasta are the best-loved foods. In fact, today was the first time in this area that I have been offered eggplant parmigiana. Parma is about 100 kilometers away, over the Appenines, in another region altogether.

After purchasing the fish, I strolled around the market and found a stall selling shoes made in Italy. Since I have an aversion to leather shoes made in China, this was heaven. I bought two pairs in the same style, one in brown, the other in black, for 39 euros each, a bargain.

The villa before renovation and the hillside of rubble

The store-keeper inspected both several times to make sure they were a matching pair, trimmed off any stray threads, inspected them again, turned them upside down to check the sizes, wrapped them in tissue, returned them to their original boxes, and gratefully accepted a local check without asking for identification. As the town clock stuck half past 12, we realized we were late for lunch and we raced back along the mountain road to get to Spino Fiorito (translation as best as we can figure out: The Flowering Thorn, something to do with the Malaspina family from centuries ago) for lunch with our crew.

Now, fully refuelled, we can return to the *campo*, the field, and continue cutting and raking the hay and weeds into piles to be burned when the sun has sufficiently dried them out. Our perilously steep hillside is slowly taking shape. Though there are some parcels of land we have yet failed to find, we are at present focusing on those we can see from our windows and which will eventually become my hillside garden. Previously, it had been a hillside of rubbish, literally—it was where the neighbors had thrown their refuse over many years.

Meanwhile, the *ragazzi*, the guys, return to their current project of figuring out how to build a flight of stone steps from the upper patio down to the garden level. The planning stage has taken six months; I realize it has taken that long because they haven't yet figured out quite how to do it. Marco, the *geometra*—which is a cross between an architect and a surveyor—has been called in yet again. The entire crew paces about with tape measures and bits of string, clambering up on boulders, measuring and gesticulating and arguing and finally a hole is dug and concrete is poured. It will be like this, *cosi*, they say. Then, *non, cosi,* the plan has changed. This is a public way, they suddenly discover, and the steps cannot descend *cosi,* like this, but must be *cosi,* like that! Unfortunately, I have to leave the country on Saturday, so I fear I will not see the finished staircase this trip. I am disappointed but know that the sooner I leave, the sooner I can return to

**Work on the
steps continues**

this magical place and see the completed project. I know our *ragazzi* will do a good job, I trust them completely—they have turned our sad pile of stones into an enchanting place and their love for this historic building is almost as great as ours.

This afternoon we will sign the contract with Marco for work to commence on the downstairs floors , which will give us another complete apartment with three bedrooms and three bathrooms, so this house will sleep 12 in all. This work is due to be finished by April, and then they will start work on the pool, which will be quite a feat, considering that our hillside is almost vertical.

Later that evening, I discovered an exquisite shiny black scorpion in the bathroom. I captured it in a glass, intending to release it outside, but sadly it stung itself and so I flushed it down the toilet. I don't think nature has ever created anything quite so glitteringly black and evil looking as a scorpion, though the neighbors tell me the sting is no worse than a bee sting.

View of the side of the villa showing the completed steps

Letter to My Daughter Tessa

Easter 2005

Dear Tessa,

I thought I should send you a bulletin from Italy, along with some photos, because things are starting to happen here, in fact, since Easter Monday (a holiday) it's been all systems go. Today at 8 am, Stefano and Massimo arrived to start mixing the cement for the retaining wall for the swimming pool terrace (finally!), Riccardo and Gabriele arrived to rebuild the roof on the old wood shed, and Daniele the electrician arrived with his mate to put air conditioners in both bedrooms. Ginny and Gary were here Monday and Tuesday night and left on Wednesday, which was the craziest day, with Carmello the plumber and his helper climbing all over the roof putting up the solar panels for hot water, the same day as two men were putting in the screens on the French windows and installing the new windows in the barn. And just as they we driving away, the man from the nursery in Pallerone arrived to deliver the olive tree I had bought—so it was all systems go. And then Carmello turned off the hot water by mistake, so it's just as well that Gary and Ginny left, because I don't think they'd appreciate cold showers.

It's so exciting seeing this finally taking shape, to see my vision becoming a reality. It really is a gem of a place, a work of art, as Gary called it. We have been having big lunches at Spino Fiorito every day, and the food is getting even better, though Stefano won't eat there, he says it's too rich, and prefers to go to Il Re di Macchia in Casola, which is way too plain for me. Although, the past couple of days, while it's just been him and Massimo, they've been going to Massimo's home in the next village for a home-cooked meal by his mother—I asked them if we could all come along too!

Today, Riccardo and Gabriele are putting up the pergola over the outdoor dining table, and yesterday we went to Sarzana to buy a large terracotta pot and wisteria to grow over it. It's all going to look so pretty when things start growing. We are obviously in a heat wave, with more than two weeks with no rain, and it gets hotter each day. Great if you are on vacation, but not so good if you are growing things. Maurizio shakes his head and stands in the shade, saying it's bad for the earth. He is thinking of his new Merlot grapes that he planted in March.

And on top of all this, Ron's furniture arrived from the US a week ago. The container was delivered, just as it had been packed in Boston, and was parked at the end of our lane. The shippers had a small van which they loaded with crates and drove up and down the lane to the storage space we had prepared underneath the big barn. One of the white rabbits that our neighbor's grandson was given for Easter was running all around that morning, it was so cute—he lives in Lina's chicken coop but had managed to escape. So that took all morning, and when we went down to Lo Spino, all the removal men were down there tucking into their lunch! What a great job they did; they earned a good lunch.

We have put a few things of Ron's in the house, but not a lot because the house was pretty much perfect before, but we did rearrange the guest bedroom, because the olive chest that was in there was a bit too big; we put a chest of drawers and a mirror there instead, I'll send a photo. Lina unfortunately has been in New Jersey with relatives all this time, so I haven't seen her, and I miss her, but I'm glad she wasn't here when her wall fell down! I think that's all sorted out now, and things are back on schedule.

I must go out and see how things are progressing with the pergola. It's so great being here, I've never had such good weather before. But I'll be home this time next week—I get in at 3 pm on Thursday via Air France, if you can pick me up that would be great—but I have a very tight connection, so please check to make sure that I get on that plane. If I don't I'll try and call you or Ron.

Have a great weekend, hope it's warmed up there by now!

Much love, Mom xxx

Power to the People

Earth Day, April 2008

I WAS PERUSING THE BUSINESS PAGES of the *International Herald Tribune* the other day when two contiguous articles caught my eye. It seemed to me they might be related.

One was titled, "Nestle chairman keeps his eye on the future," and quoted him as saying that Nestle, the largest food manufacturer in the world, with 2007 revenues of $108 billion, was looking to "wellness and nutrition" products to propel their profit margins ever higher. No, they weren't planning new products they thought would benefit us nutritionally, they were aiming to increase their profits by "playing to the fashion for health and diet." So health and diet are a fashion, a fad? I think they may be wrong there. It's more likely that we the people are trying to counteract the adverse effects of highly processed and packaged so-called "foods" in favor of healthy whole foods that will keep us healthy. The link between high-calorie processed foods and such diseases as diabetes, cancer and heart disease, as well as obesity, has been proven beyond a doubt. Maybe this "fashion" is the result of the US population making an attempt to reclaim their access to healthy food, the kind of food we used to eat 50 years ago, before Agribusiness started processing and packaging and advertising these products. Though they do taste good. They make sure of this by adding chemical flavorings, artificial sweeteners, and "food enhancers," such as MSG, which has recently been found to be highly addictive and have dire side-effects in certain people.

The other article's headline read, "For U.S. shoppers, bare essentials." The first line of the article reads: "Americans are cutting back on purchases of things they do not have to have, sending retail sales down sharply." The article explained that while dollars spent on food in March 2008 had risen 4.3 percent, they had fallen up to 7 percent on a variety of consumer products. Well, I thought, this might be good news. Maybe we have all tired of that cheap crap, the kind you can buy at the Christmas Tree Shops, or Home Goods, or Marshalls, made in China by underpaid labor of materials of dubious origins (sustainable hardwoods? I think not); the kind that looks chintzy or falls apart after a few uses, ends up at the dump, and soon after is on a boat loaded with refuse headed for some third-world country all too happy to buy our garbage. Maybe we all have had our fill of buying all this "stuff," and have realized that it really doesn't enhance our lives, that actually it complicates them. One of the largest growing small businesses now is building storage units so people have more space to keep the stuff they don't have room for in their houses. My hope is that our population is realizing we don't need all this stuff, and that maybe it's better to spend our money on buying better food, food that nourishes us and keeps us healthy, so we don't end up with diabetes or cancer or heart disease. Or makes us obese. And by buying organic food, we also support the smaller family-run farms which are using farming techniques that are safer for our land and water supply, not to mention the actual food itself.

I have always believed that the power is with the people, and that our vote counts and that we must vote with our pocket book. Every penny we spend in the stores counts. If we don't buy junk food and cheap plastic goods from China and DO buy quality goods and healthy, organic food, we not only benefit, but the earth benefits, the world benefits. If no one buys Coco Pops, not only will we have healthier children, but Kelloggs will go bankrupt. Now THAT'S power!

Seeking Sacred Space in Italy

I WANDERED INTO a beautiful church yesterday, more like a small basilica, really, in Busto Arsizio, the small town on the outskirts of Milan where Ron's uncle Petronio lives. Each church I visit in Italy amazes me. They all have their own character—some masculine, and some, like this one, so feminine I imagine it's like being in a womb. This one is dedicated to San Giuseppe, and it was hard to believe it was built and designed by men. Outside, the facade is a faded golden marble, but inside, it is astonishingly flesh-toned, the walls lined with blocks of granite which has been finely chiseled to give a felt-like finish in alternating colors of light pink, soft grey, and a darker, almost terra cotta color. The massive pillars on each side of the nave reach up to support extravagant baroque arches billowing high above, and every inch of ceiling is painted with scenes of cherubs and angels cavorting against a blue sky. The altarpiece, instead of a gruesome crucifix, is like a Dresden centerpiece, four-sided, about 20 feet high, a confection of white marble figures, angels and curlicues piled on top. Every available space was decorated with masses of white lilies and tiny pink carnations, probably for a wedding, or maybe for the funeral that I sat in on, though I think probably not. If the designers of this sacred space had intended to create an impression of heaven, they succeeded, as I had a profound emotional response, the kind that art often provokes, where I feel I'm either going to throw up or burst into tears.

I first realized the power of sacred space when I visited Assisi in 2001. I was not on a pilgrimage of any sort, just a tourist, getting re-acquainted with Italy after a 30 year hiatus. In fact, if it had not been teeming with rain that day, we probably wouldn't haven't visited the Basilica of San Francesco at all, viewing it as a tourist trap. But since we were there, why not? So we hailed a cab and joined the throng of Italian pilgrims intent on touching the tomb of St. Francis and viewing his "treasure," his worldly belongings. But I was completely unprepared for the sense of love and piety that was palpable on descending into the old *chiesa*. It was more like a cave than a church, which are usually designed to reach for the heavens. This had low, curved arches, every inch decorated with ancient frescos, many by Giotto. The lack of windows created a closeness in the air and there was a sense of profound peace, a true refuge from the frenetic world beyond the walls. I know I'm not alone in having this reaction—others have told me that they, too, wandered through this holy place with tears running down their cheeks. This is indeed a sacred space, filled with beauty, created with love, to offer comfort to all who seek it. This kind of feeling transcends religion, it is a universal gift, and I was awed to realize that the love and inspiration of St. Francis and St. Clare could still be felt 800 years later, that it was their influence, their love, we were being touched by.

On the same trip, I had visited Siena, a magical medieval city with an imposing *duomo* (cathedral) built of black and white marble. Inside, there is more black and white marble, with portraits of a succession of popes arranged around the top of the massive pillars. Marble floors, marble walls, marble altars—hard edges everywhere, and many carvings of saints and popes and crucifixes, definitely a masculine place. I felt not a frisson of awe or peace visiting this place; it was obviously built as a display of wealth and power, not so much to glorify God but to outdo Florence and Lucca, Siena's rivals. I find that the city of Florence has the same effect on me. It feels muscular, grey, masculine, all about money, business, and power. After all, Florence gave us the idea and name for a bank. I feel uncomfortable there, and have yet to feel my soul stir in Florence. Though it houses a fifth of the world's art treasures, they are mostly hidden away in museums, palaces and churches, and one is left to wander the narrow city streets and dark alleys searching for a glimmer of charm in some secluded courtyard through locked iron gates. Maybe it's the hoards of tourists and American coeds, but Florence is not an easy city to penetrate, and sacred space seems in short supply. Goethe felt the same way; he said in his

Italian diaries, "I did not wish to stay long . . . I hurried out of the city as quickly as I had entered it."

Then there's the church in Codiponte, a little village near ours, which is built in the early Romanesque style on the site of a Roman temple. It is unadorned, with walls of plain stone, and has startlingly explicit carvings of fertility symbols decorating the capitols that church officials seem to have turned a blind eye to; an interesting place, but again lacking in any sense of the mystical. [This is where our neighbor Amadeo had his funeral service as our church was damaged by the earthquake in 2013]

It seems to be in the more humble places that one feels one's soul stir, often in simple churches decorated by artists and artisans, most anonymous, whose only goal is to create a place of comfort and beauty. I am thinking of the church in Sarzana I visited by chance. A fire long ago destroyed the decorative plaster interior so it now resembles a protestant church with bare stone walls. It seems very sparse, naked almost. But halfway down on the left-hand side there is a statue of

Interior of a chapel in Fivizzano

Jesus of Nazareth, about seven feet high, carved out of rich chestnut wood, with arms outstretched and a look of compassion on His face. It is a true work of art, though the artist is unknown. I can only say that standing there, admiring the quality of the carving, I suddenly felt as if I were about to be taken into His arms and comforted, and that too, was an experience that touched my heart. In this unadorned church, there was the very essence of the teachings of Jesus—love and compassion.

The little church next to our house in the tiny village of Reusa is another such place. Modest and simple, it serves to mark the passing of time with baptisms, weddings, and more often these days, funerals, for this small and dwindling mountain community. The women of the village—Lina, Rosetta, Lida, Meralda, and Carla—gather every Friday afternoon per *pulire la chiesa,* to clean the church. It only gets used for half an hour a week, on Saturday afternoons, when the priest, who has so many villages to take care of he can't get to all of them on a Sunday, arrives in his little van and rushes into the church to perform a somewhat perfunctory mass. But the women scrub and polish the little church, covering surfaces with white lace, adding arrangements of wild flowers and the odd potted plant, and filling it with love. They have made it into a womb-like space, a sanctuary to escape from the rigors and hardships of everyday life, a place of peace.

I love to go to services at this church which is the heart of the village, but do find them somewhat lacking in spiritual quality, all that alternating sitting and standing and muttering and chanting with the priest rushing through the mass. What moves me more is to spend half an hour lying in the grass in the olive grove, nestled among buttercups and clover, listening to the call of the cuckoo and the cow bells gently clanging in the distance. This for me is a truly sacred place, a place where I can be totally present and give thanks for this gift of being able to experience the world as a truly beautiful, peaceful place, for finding Heaven on Earth. I think we all need a place like this.

The Church Bells

Monday, October 11th, 2009

TODAY THE BELLS STARTED to chime at 10:15 am. At first I thought it was for a church service; after all, last week they suddenly started ringing at around 3:30 on Tuesday afternoon, and it was only when I saw Lina afterwards that she told me that it was for the rescheduled Saturday service, already rescheduled from Sunday, because the priest now has too many churches and parishes to get around to. Apparently he had been sick and the only day he could come was Tuesday. Heart problems, apparently, and by the size of him, I am not surprised. For a while, he had taken to having lunch at our local restaurant, and his presence on a Friday meant that Davide had to make sure we had fish for lunch. Not major fish, which is rare

View of the campanile from the aia (stone courtyard) of Casa della Quercia

in this part of Italy, but token fish, or even just a gesture, like throwing a few anchovies into the pasta sauce, though sometimes we were lucky enough to have stuffed mussels or *spaghetti alle vongole*.

But these bells sounded different—a couple of deep bongs, then a flurry of notes from the two higher-octave bells, followed by a paroxysm, almost a tune, from all three of them. I looked up to the top of the campanile, the bell tower, and saw a man wearing gigantic ear muffs swinging the bells back and forth, getting right inside them and having a good look at the clappers, making sure all was in order. I took a photo and went to fetch some logs for the fire—it feels a bit nippy today—when I saw Emma, Miralda's mother, walking by. We exchanged greetings and I asked her what was going on. About once a year, she tells me, they come to check the bells. Ah, so that's what it's all about!

I make sure to tell her that we do like the bells. *Que belle campane!* I tell her. I am a bit worried that the villagers think we DON'T like them, since we once sent around a petition to have them silenced at night. I feel I must explain that they would ring twice, because our elderly neighbor Roberto, Lina's husband, who was the church warden at the time, told us he never would hear them the first time. When he was out in the fields or his olive grove, he'd want to know what time it was, but the first time they rang, he'd forget to start counting. His answer to this problem was to set the mechanism to ring twice, the first time to get him to pay attention, and the second to give him time to start to count the hour. Unfortunately for us, the bell that chimed the half hour was badly cracked. So in the middle of night, for instance at 12:30, we'd get twelve loud bongs and then a nasty, dull clank for the half hour, and then two minutes later, the whole performance would start all over again—and so on all through the night. I liked to joke, Let's buy them all clocks and wristwatches and stop the bells! But when Roberto died suddenly, just a year after we had arrived, no one had the heart to change the bell-ringing schedule. It stayed that way for about five years, but the Powers That Be seemed to have heard of our discontent, and the Belle Arti, or maybe the Church, or both, came with a big flourish to Reusa and dismantled the entire mechanism, refurbished the bells, and replaced the cracked half-hour bell at considerable trouble and expense. So now we hear a more mellifluous bonging and clanging every half hour during the day—but during the night, after 9 and before 7, the half-hour is marked by a single clang, which is so much better for a good night's sleep. Even though it's illegal—the new law in Italy says that no bells are to ring at night—and we could make a fuss about it, but actually, we like it. In fact, we have come to love the bells. And so we keep quiet about it. But we are grateful that half-past midnight is no longer such a rousing affair.

View of campanile and church from the meadow

Artists Always Find the Best Places

c. 2010

ON SATURDAY we were invited to dine with an artist who is renovating an old house and barn near Licciano Nardi. I had heard much about Barry John Raybold and the massive project he's working on—an entire hill top! with no electricity! and no water!—but had never met him, and was looking forward to doing so since he had studied with Cedric Egeli, who himself had studied with Henry Hensche in Provincetown. Right now he's living in an apartment in La Serra, next to Lerici on the Mediterranean coast, while his project is being completed—two years now with no end in sight.

We drove there after spending an afternoon in Sarzana in the department store buying beds and mattresses and were ready for a change of scenery. As always, we were stunned by the breathtakingly beautiful views of the Mediterranean as we drove along the coast road and up to the town perched high above the Golfo dei Poeti. Named for Lord Byron, who famously swam across the Gulf of La Spezia from Lerici to Portovenere, and also for his friend Shelley, who drowned while out sailing Byron's boat, this area is, I think, one of the world's great beauty spots. It never fails to grab at my heart, that first glimpse of the blue Mediterranean, the bougainvillea-clad villas clinging to the steep hillsides, the landscape luxuriously cushioned with mounded green bushes of laurel and ilex and punctuated with cypress trees. Long-past memories, perhaps time-echoes, flash through my mind and I imagine Phoenicians, Saracens and Crusaders plying these waters in their wooden ships, navigating the rocky cliffs and inlets with ancient instruments, intent on trading and warring and looting, and converting the heathens.

Barry's apartment was on the top floor of an old, tall building opposite the church at La Serra, right next to a wide paved courtyard overlooking the bay. I imagine the town would hold their *festas* here, with music and food and dancing into the late hours under a starry sky and this incredible view spread out before them. We arrived at dusk after the sun had just set and turned the panorama a misty pink. It was indescribably beautiful, the sort of view that brings tears to your eyes. I have had many such experiences in Italy, and I realized this morning, thinking about that view and how much I love the Mediterranean coast, that I experience Italy with my heart, not my head. Last fall when I arrived at Pisa airport, I found myself unexpectedly tearing up as I walked through the cool marble halls of the airport; this time I arrived, the tears came as the plane landed. It's a sense of release, of relief at having arrived at this special land where life is lived differently. I used to think that my intellect isn't exercised enough here—although speaking Italian is certainly an intellectual challenge—but in fact, experiencing life from the heart is how we SHOULD experience it, it's how the human race lived and survived for millennia, something so many of us have forgotten. And I am so glad that I have not only the opportunity to live that way, if only for part of the year, but also to be aware, to be appreciative, of that fact.

View of the Bay of La Spezia from La Serra

Italy is A-Changing

Thursday, Sept. 30th, 2010

I HAVE NOT WRITTEN about Italy in some years, which is a shame, I think, since our little community is changing—Italy is changing, and the world is changing, slowly but surely. We all try to hang onto something that is timeless. My life in Italy feels that way—until one of our neighbors dies.

Gilberto succumbed this past winter, and many of the others are in their 70s and 80s. Before things change more, I feel the urge to write down some thoughts, to maybe make time stand still. But I hesitate to do so. So much has been written about Italy, maybe too much—about ancient houses being restored, about fine romances, wine being made, olives being crushed, and amusingly eccentric workmen being charmingly stubborn. All of these I can write about, except perhaps the fine romance.

But I want to tell of simpler things, gentler things. Like the weather and seasons. We don't have "weather" here, not like we do in New England. Here, in Italy, either there's a brief storm, or it's still, with not a leaf moving; day after day of shimmering stillness, the kind of stillness where you can lie on the grass and feel the thrum of nature, the heartbeat of an organism in harmony with Spirit, as if you can hear things grow. In the summer, the air seems palpable, golden, as if you could scoop it up in your hand. They say it's due to the fine sand blown in from the Sahara on the southwest wind. This morning I woke up at five a.m. and looked out at the darkness to see moon shadows outlining trees and hedges and hillsides. There was absolute stillness and silence except for owls hooting in the chestnut woods and rushing water in the streams, swollen from a recent rain fall. I noticed the sentinels of the cypress trees I have planted through the years, seven of them now, after one was nibbled to death by a herd of goats. How they have grown. What an honor, and a responsibility, I thought, to be able to make such a mark on the landscape. I make a mental note to buy more trees and get out the pick axe once again. Ah, clay soil! Sometimes I wish for the sandy soil of Cape Cod.

One can observe the seasons change, slowly and inexorably, as they are supposed to. Spring isn't a no-show, as it often is in New England, when we tend to emerge from a very long, chilly winter into sudden summer. But now, summer is sliding into distant memory; chestnut leaves are crisping on the trees, mushrooms are springing up everywhere, and piles of neatly chopped wood are appearing outside cottages, covering entire outside walls. Crickets are making their last feeble chirps, and branches hang heavy with a bumper crop of olives and apples. The country roads, as usual at this time of year, are cushioned with a layer of squashed chestnuts, walnuts and figs, which have plummeted down from overhanging trees.

But mostly it's the people, our neighbors, that make life in the village of Reusa such a sweet experience. Simple country folk, most of the men war veterans, they follow the rhythms of the earth, planting by the waxing moon. They live off the land, taking full advantage of what Nature has to offer—growing vegetables in their *orto*, hunting for fungi in secret mossy places, collecting chestnuts and walnuts to sell by the sack in the fall, gathering olives in winter, and, of course, making their own wine, a point of fierce pride for all Italian men.

Our neighbors Rosetta and Amadeo told me today that their son Marcello will come tomorrow from Tunisia with his wife and son to help with the *vendemmia*, the grape harvest. He is a geologist for an oil company. Their other son Duilio will arrive soon after. When Amadeo has finished his harvest, he will bring his grinder with a long pipe over to his sister's house, our next door neighbor Lina, and her sons will help her harvest the grapes and then grind them; the purple grape juice will be piped into the cantina, into a huge oak cask that was built by her husband's grandfather. Her son Maurizio makes wine the old fashioned way, he learned the skill from his father of listening for a change in the bubbling sound of the fermenting grapes. Every day he comes to the cantina to listen until he decides it's time to decant the wine into demijohns with a tap. The wine is never bottled, we fill up old empty wine bottles straight from the tap (yes, we have a key to their cellar). No additives, no preservatives, no clarifiers. It is in fact the only wine I can drink, it tastes like pure nectar. But this is not a good year for wine. There is much shaking of jowls and sucking of teeth as the *contadini* discuss the weather—the summer was not sunny enough, they say; or there was too much rain; or a late September hailstorm broke some of the skins. On a good year they'll worry that the wild boar will get into the vineyards to munch on the grapes. Maurizio once stayed up all night with a shotgun to protect his grapes the day before the harvest.

So it is that at this time of year the narrow country roads are clogged by men on tractors and *api*, small three-wheeled trucks powered by Vespa engines, loaded with empty oak barrels and buckets and boxes of grapes, readying themselves for the ardors of the harvest, and later, the drinking of the wine. One year recently, after a very dry summer and a good year for grapes, there was a water shortage because everyone had at the same time filled their huge oak barrels with water to swell the wood so it was ready to take the wine without leakage. No one likes to admit it, but in years like this, when the harvest is thin, they are forced to buy grapes grown in the south, shipped up here for this very purpose, to supplement their own.

· · ·

The workmen, too, have become our friends. They have been renovating our old house, on and off, and now on again, for the last seven years. They are back on the job, which means the cement mixer has taken up residence center-stage once more, and we can look forward to leisurely lunches every noon at the local restaurant. Today the guys seemed a bit subdued—the capo, the boss, Stefano, was not there, and Delio and Riccardo had had a falling out, each wanting to be boss in his place. Delio is working on the lower floor, where a staircase will descend from the new master bedroom on the middle floor. Today he was removing some stones from a wall, square stones, beautifully worked, typical of Roman foundations. The mortar had dried out and you could put your hand through the gaps between the stones, where birds have been nesting in the crevices. He will fill the gaps with new mortar. It's sobering to think that these stones were cut so long ago, 1500 years at least, and then it dawns on me that they were probably worked by prisoners or slaves of the Romans, possibly British. Or Welsh. When I walk along the Roman road, the Via del Volto Santo, that goes right through our property and under our

Delio working on the Roman foundation of the villa

Ron with Mario the carpenter

ancient stone patio, my spine tingles at the thought that this was once
a thoroughfare for pilgrims 1,000 years ago, and probably before that.

Mario, the 82-year-old carpenter who is making our windows, came
by to fit the glass in the frames he had already put in place, only to
find they had been cut the wrong size. He took all the windows out,
and now has disappeared with a promise to be back on Saturday. The
middle floor is now windowless. Two steps forward, one back. Daniele the electrician arrives to help with the under floor heating in the
bathroom—why won't it work? The transformer is too small, he tells
us. He promises to get a larger one. He stays and chats with Riccardo,
they share a cigarette. Another neighbor Roberto comes by to join in
the conversation. Riccardo continues his job of tiling the floor, chatting away easily, and I am reminded once again how relaxed Italians
are. And I realize my own level of stress has lessened; I am becoming languorous, like a plump, contented hen. I think about food a
lot, about as much as the average Italian: When are we going to eat?
Where? What? How are we going to cook it? Lina always asks, What

are you cooking for dinner tonight? It's the conversation opener *dopo pranzo*, after lunch.

Another neighbor, the painter Roberto Silvestri, walks by and I ask if I can come to see his paintings, since I missed his show in Casola this past August. He invites me into the old house he and his wife rent from the Church—the new *canonica*—and I admire his work. He paints in an Eastern European style—realistic, slightly-garish paintings on the back of glass or Plexiglas panels. It is a dying art. I commission a painting of our villa from him. He is old; I am surprised to see him back in Reusa. This may be his last visit, but I hope not, he is such a nice man. On Monday their son, a professor at Bologna University, will pick them up to take them to the city for the winter. With luck they'll return again next spring. Which is when I'll return too. God willing.

I ragazzi outside Spino Fiorito:

left to right, Ron, Delio, Riccardo, Gabriele and Stefano

The Vineyard, or
The Contadino in Need of Land

Monday, October 4th, 2010

I HAVE JUST RETURNED from our neighbors Velia and Roberto's house. They hi-jacked me after lunch with a gift of a freshly picked *porcino* mushroom the size of a dinner place, and then invited me into their house for some *frittata delle gallette*, made of wild mushrooms, which we—and the French—call chanterelles. Of course, there was the obligatory glass of homemade wine to go with it—it would be rude to refuse—and then the offer of *limoncino*. *No, grazie, non posso!* No, I couldn't possibly, I say—but again, it would be rude to refuse, so I sample a thimble-full, inhaling the lemony scent and taking the tiniest drop onto my lips to savor the tart-sweet taste. I never could understand the Italian obsession with growing lemon trees, but now I understand—making *limoncino* comes second only to making wine in the pantheon of truly manly activities, Italian style, except, maybe, for shooting small song birds with a 12-bore shotgun.

Velia then recounts their special recipe for *limoncino*: start with a liter of 95 percent proof alcohol, add an equal amount of water—it must be spring water, from the village fountain—then add sugar, I forget how much, a kilo I think—then the grated zest of 12 lemons, but with absolutely none of the white bits, add a handful of some type of dried herbs, with a pinch of saffron, and let marinate for 45 days. I realize I need to have them to write it down for me to make sure I get it right. Then the conversation turns to the lemon trees themselves. Roberto has suggested we plant some in the most perfect spot in Reusa for lemon trees—the south-facing terrace below our swimming pool. We might have to plant them in pots, he explains, and then move them into the pool house for the winter. They would water them when they needed it.

The conversation, fueled and emboldened by the liquor, veers suddenly to what's really on their minds—a vineyard. On our land. On our land which has just been cleared at considerable expense and which is now, as they say, *vuoto*, empty. To an Italian that is sacrilege. Roberto suggests white grapes to make the local Candia wine. We must get the land leveled and tilled, have the soil analyzed to apply for an official DOC permit, buy the vines, plant them during the waxing moon in February, and put a fence around it. That's all. It would be quite simple. And he'd help us make the wine. Oh, and one more thing. We need to get some sheep, maybe goats, or even a donkey, maybe two, to eat the grass around the vines and under the olive trees. It would mean less tedious work with the *cespuliatore*, that accursed backbreaking gasoline-powered giant of a weed-whacker with its fierce metal blade. It would be like having four-legged lawn mowers. Velia and Roberto would feed the animals in the winter, even make a little house for them in the field, give them hay. They are both talking at me at once. In Italian. My brain feels numb and I fail to find the words for "I'll think about it and get back to you." It's a good idea, I think to myself, but I'm only here two or three months a year . . . and Ron, who lives here all year, is not, let's say, nature's child. He is a city kid. But he's learning. Then they add, as if to convince me, A donkey will be fun for the guests! Their children will love to take rides! I immediately think about liability insurance. And I imagine donkeys running wild and goats leaping over fences and eating my cherished cypress trees and terraced herb gardens. I struggle to find the words for, "Let me take a nap and mull it over," a phrase I haven't yet formulated in Italian. I take my leave, loaded down with the huge *porcino*, a slice of the *frittata*, a bag full of ripe tomatoes, and a pot of this season's blackberry jam.

A few days later, walking back from our local restaurant after another leisurely lunch with the workers, I run into Velia by the cemetery, about halfway between the restaurant and our village. It is a beautiful sunny day, and she and Roberto are working in an olive grove way down the hillside, cleaning it for Sergio's sister. Sergio Bacci is now Il Capo of the village since our neighbor Roberto died in 2004. He has a cow shed next to his house where he keeps about a couple of cows who provide several calves a year and milk all year round, which many people in the village buy from him. It is not legal to keep a cow in the center of the village, but no one says anything. He's been doing it for years, as did his father and grandfather before him. The laws might change, but not the local customs. Plus, everyone has something to hide, we have discovered—maybe an illegal bit (*abusivo*) added on to their house or barn, or something that needs a permit that hasn't got one, or they are earning a living that is heavily cash-based and therefore tax-free. We have learned it's best to keep quiet about these things. I vaguely remember something about people who live in glass houses should not throw stones . . .

But the main reason Sergio has cows, it seems to me, is that they provide him with his own personal supply of *concime*, cow manure, to spread on his *orto*, his vegetable garden, and, more importantly, his vineyard and his olive trees. Everyone is jealous of his plentiful supply of cow manure, but no one else wants to go to the bother of actually keeping cows any more. Roberto and Velia keep a small *orto* on his land and this evening when I went by to pick some radicchio, I saw a mound of still-smoking cow manure ready to be spread under the fading tomato vines and bean poles. It did occur to me to skim off a bucket for the three olive trees we keep in large pots on the terrace, and which are always desperate for some serious nutrition, but decide being branded as a thief is too high a price to pay.

Velia beckons me down the hill so I clamber down the old mountain track in my city shoes—it's Tuesday, market day in Fivizzano, so I had dressed up a bit—to make a good impression, *fare una bella figura*—and gone there that morning to visit the market and to withdraw from the bank a huge sum in cash for our workers because, this being Italy, everyone gets paid in *contanti*, cash. It's quite normal. That way we can avoid paying tax. We also have no record of how much it's costing us to renovate this house, but apparently that doesn't matter either.

I skitter down the path and find Roberto cutting grass with a large *cespuliatore*, sweating profusely, happy as a, well, a *contadino* working his land. He shows me mud puddles where the wild boar like to come to wallow in the night, and tells me how many olives the trees will yield when they have finished cleaning and pruning them. Cutting the grass is always called cleaning, just as olive trees are called plants, *piante*, not trees.

Roberto and Velia measuring the meadow for a vineyard

a house in Morocco and an apartment on the sea front in Marina di Carrarra, about an hour away. I asked Roberto why they preferred to live in a small rented cottage, owned by their friend Sergio, way up in these mountains? He explained that he can't live in the city, and, putting his hands around his neck, made a graphic choking sound. It reminded me of why I had left London, abandoning my spacious rent-controlled Chelsea apartment for a new life on Cape Cod. But I could never explain it as well as he did. Italians have such a gift for expressing themselves with their hands. I can learn a lot from them.

Velia tells me they are cleaning this land because it's their passion. They love living the life of traditional *contadini*, growing their own food, foraging in the forest for wild greens in the springtime and mushrooms in the fall, cutting wood for their fire, and tending olives trees for their friends and neighbors. When they do, they get half the olive oil, it's the old *mezzadria* system. But they also do it because Sergio's sister is old and lives in Genoa and if the land isn't cleaned there is a fine, and then the land can be considered abandoned. So they feel it is their duty, as members of the extended Bacci family, to help out.

Suddenly Roberto gets very agitated. He is upset that Pierino, who we hired to clean our olive grove, didn't turn up once this summer to cut the grass. It needs to be done at least twice a season, he says. And this year there is a bumper crop of olives. It annoys him no end that Pierino will reap the benefit of the olive harvest with almost no work. I decide not to remind him that Pierino had pruned the olive trees the year before, an arduous task, which may be the reason why they are now loaded with olives. We have already told Roberto that he can take care of our olive grove next year. By law, the contract to tend an olive grove, a verbal one, must be honored for two years, so it's Pierino's for another few months. But Roberto knows that next year the crop will be meager, as it always is after a good year. So much work for so little olive oil!

Then the conversation turns to The Vineyard. Had I thought about it? Did I think it was a good idea? Yes, I said, let's talk more. So we agree to have lunch together on Thursday to talk it over.

The next day, I hear Maurizio trundling by on his tractor loaded with empty demijohns and follow him into his mother's cantina (wine cellar.) There I see Lina turning the screw on a wine press, squeezing the last purple juice from the grapes of the first pressing. They offer me a glass of last year's wine, which is delicious, as always. I ask if it's San Giovese. Yes, they say, but there's also some *ciliegiollo* grapes in there, and also some *tose*, which are traditional in this area. In fact, the local government is giving out grants for people to plant vineyards of these heritage grapes. My ears prick up and I take another mouthful of the wine. Not complicated, but fruity, with a definite flavor of cherries, minimal oak or tannin undertones, and enough body that you can almost chew it. This is my kind of wine! Yes, I would love to grow these old-fashioned grapes.

**Lina and her son Maurizio in their cantina squeezing
the last drops of juice from their grapes**

At lunch the next day I ask Delio, who is a keen gardener, what he thinks of the local *ciliegiollo* grape. He surprises me by saying that growing grapes for wine takes too much time, it's better to grow olives, you just cut the grass a few times a year, collect the olives, take them to the *frantoio*, the olive mill, and that's it. But, I point out, brandishing a glass of local table wine, you can't drink it, like this. The others at the table agree. Riccardo, who loves his wine, says that making olive oil is far too much work, growing vines is much easier. He remembers going to the olive mill to get the olives crushed, after backbreaking work picking them, and there was such a back log that he fell asleep in the truck. They finally got their olives crushed in the middle of the night. He figures it takes a week for two people to pick enough olives to make up one *quintale*, 100 kilos, which yields about 23 to 24 kilos of oil. It costs 20 euro to crush a *quintale* of olives, and a kilo of oil equals 750 cl. So basically, you'd end up with about 24 large bottles of unfiltered, extra-virgin olive oil. Is it worth it all the labor? It obviously depends on who is doing the picking.

Thursday, October 14th

Thursday lunchtime—*ora di pranzo*— is heralded by the newly-adjusted Church bell, which now rings on time, and we all set off to the local watering hole, Spino Fiorito, for lunch. We are seven in all, but if you count the number of people in the restaurant who were included in our lunchtime conversation, I would say it was about 20. Our neighbors Velia and Roberto were full of lively conversation. I learned that Velia's uncle was Chamberlain to the King of Morocco, and that her father went to work there too, after he had been released after six or seven years of captivity by the British in the Sudan after the war. This sounded unlikely to me, but I didn't want to dwell on possible British war atrocities. One so often has the fond idea that one's own kind act like gentlemen during wartime when other nationalities act like barbarians, but sadly this is often not the case. Anyway, this is how she has ended up with a house in Tangiers. We talked about our favorite places in Morocco, the best way to drive to Nice, where we were planning to go for the weekend, the best restaurants along our eastern-most stretch of the Riviera, which were our favorite towns in the Cinque Terre and the best ways to get to them, and the rise of materialism in Italian society. Meanwhile, I couldn't help but notice that Riccardo had drunk an entire bottle of white wine, twice what he usually drinks for lunch. This observation haunted me later in the afternoon when he made a mistake while laying the floor tiles in a herringbone pattern—on the straight he was fine, but he had got lost in the eddies and back-waters of the twisting corridor between the kitchen and bedroom. It can be a dangerous time, *dopo pranzo*, after lunch.

After two hours and several bottles of wine, we realized we hadn't yet broached the subject of the vineyard with Velia and Roberto. So we agree to get together for dinner at our place that evening, pooling our food—pot-luck Italian style—and we will *chiachiereremo*, we will chat, said Velia. The next person who tells me that English is a difficult language to learn will get a smack around the head. For the future tense of a verb, all we have to do is insert "will" between the subject and the verb. In Italian, "I will chat" is *chiachiererò*, "you (singular, informal) will chat" is *chiachiererai*, "he or she will chat" (or even more confusing, you formal) is *chiachiererà*. And don't even get me started on the subjunctive, of which there are four different tenses. Yes, English pronunciation can be a challenge, but the grammar is so easy it makes you want to weep when confronted with all 16 tenses of an Italian verb.

Potluck dinner, Italian style

At 7:30 on the dot Velia and Roberto arrive at our kitchen door laden down with platters and bottles and bags. Nothing is left to chance— they have also brought their own wine, olive oil, and bread. We are instructed to sprinkle a foil-wrapped portion of chopped dried wild marjoram on Velia's tomato salad. We add our prosciutto to their platter of sliced salami, brought at the *salumeria* in Monte Fiore in the Garfagnana—the best in the area, according to Roberto. There is a big skillet of sautéed beet greens, fresh from the *orto*, a dish of yellow and red peppers, another of baby zucchini, and a hunk of raw *pecorino* (unpasteurized sheep cheese). The wine, Roberto explained, is from Sergio's grapes and was bottled on the night of the last full moon, when the natural fermentation process gets a little boost from Mother Nature, producing a potent *frizzante*. It bubbled into our wine glasses like cherry soda. For dessert, Velia had baked a tray of tiny red apples in her wood stove; they were delicious, fluffy inside and caramelized on the outside. She explained they are called *rotelle*, roughly translated as ball-bearings or castors, being about three inches in diameter and completely round. She laughed at our enjoyment, telling us that they were from our own tree! That one, *la-giu*, down there, she said, pointing vaguely into the valley. And while we were mentally down there, trying to locate this particular apple tree in our minds, Roberto seized the opportunity to announce that the olive tree next to this particular apple tree was bearing a crop of very large, plump olives. He doesn't miss a thing. Would it be all right, he asked, if he picked them for salting and bottling, as table olives for us? I could see the wheels in his mind turning; this way, he was thinking, Pierino wouldn't get all the olives. Yes, of course, we said, anything to keep the peace. That settled, he decided we should roast chestnuts as a finale to our meal. I proudly fetched a bowl of the large chestnuts I'd gathered that day from the old tree near our departed neighbor Gilberto's house, across the valley in Montenara (one of the the five hamlets that make up the village of Reusa), only to be told by Roberto that they were too big! Big ones are better boiled, he said, the smaller ones are better roasted. Who knew? So off he dashed to his cottage next door and returned with a large plastic bag full of small, round chestnuts and a roasting pan. In just a few minutes over the kitchen fire they were roasted to perfection. This reminds me of Christmas, I said. They were surprised. When chestnut season ends, around *Tutti Santi*, November 1st, that's it for the year; Italians don't eat chestnuts after that, apparently.

And now the conversation—finally—turns to the vineyard. I mention the idea of planting *ciliegiollo* grapes, with help from the local
government, and it's not met with a lot of enthusiasm. Roberto
mentions Cabernet Sauvignon. Now I see he has something a little
more sophisticated in mind than the traditional local wine. I begin to
wonder if we are going to be able to find some common ground. But
to be honest, after all the good food and wine that day, both at lunch
and dinner, and putting in a full day's work with the builders, we
retired for the night not knowing what we had decided. Were we going ahead? Who was paying for what? Were we paying Roberto? We
have no idea! The next day we were to leave for Nice to visit friends,
so we'd have to wait to find out when we returned.

Tuesday, October 26th 2010

The workmen are not here today, since the house is more or less
finished, at least until the electrician and plumber turn up to move
things along a bit, so we meet Velia and Roberto, all bundled up
in arctic gear, to survey the prospective vineyard. At the market in
Fivizzano this morning the wind, the tramonto, was fierce and chilly,
howling down from the Alps via the Passo del Ceretto. It's always
cold in Fizizzano, say our neighbors, and they can't understand why
we go there for the market—what's wrong with Castelnuovo? Or
Aulla? But we have a fondness for the town, with its beautiful medieval square surrounded by cafes.

Down in our meadow, it's sunny and warm; the pass over the Alps at
the top of our valley, the Passo dei Carpinelli, faces south so we don't
get the same wind as the valley further north. Roberto paces and
gesticulates, demonstrating where we can level the land, he thinks
right up to where Sebastiano's *orto* ends. What about down there,
I ask, pointing to a large hollow below the olive trees; shouldn't we
plan to fill that in too? No, he says, it'll be too cold down there. That's
good for hazelnut trees and an orchard, and suggests nectarines and
peaches, though they'll take about five years before they bear fruit, he

55

cautions. Five years! I'll be old by then! But I remember that it's been eight years since we first saw this house, and time goes by so fast. They will be bearing fruit in no time. Okay, next spring we'll plant fruit and nut trees, as well as three lemon trees on the terrace by the swimming pool, and this vineyard. It's going to be a busy spring. We pace some more and figure that we have about 200 to 250 square meters of land to level; Velia calculates that we can plant about 500 vines. Five hundred! I am shocked. That seems like a lot of work. It might also mean a lot of wine. Well, not a lot, but more than I had imagined . . . and more than we can drink, just the two of us. But we could get help to drink it . . .

What about taking care of the vines, I wonder? They take care of themselves for the first three years, says Roberto. After that, you have to fence them in so the *cinghiale* (wild boar) don't eat them. And prune them. And tie them up. And spray them with copper sulfate. And then thin out the bunches of grapes. We would be glad if he would do all that work; we'll be happy to help with the *vendemmia*, and also with the drinking of the wine.

We look at the land again and wonder who we can hire to bring a bulldozer down here to level the land. Maybe Massimo, who did the heavy work required when installing the swimming pool. Then I remember the collapsed wall and realize that's not a good idea. Roberto suggests using our builders, or maybe they know someone with heavy equipment who wouldn't mind spending a morning in our field. He makes it clear that whomever we hire has to do what he says. He will be the supervisor. He even knows that word in English. Okay, we laugh, you are the supervisor! And we'll pay the bill. He is happy with that. He will take a soil sample to the DOC people and they will suggest what grapes to plant depending on the soil analysis. So we'll have to wait and see what they recommend before we know what kind of wine we'll have. I am still rooting for the cherry-flavored heritage grapes, while Roberto, I am sure, is hoping for Merlot or Cabernet Sauvignon.

We take some "before" photographs to mark the occasion and joke that we'll take "after" photographs when we open our first bottle of wine. They invite me into their cottage for a glass of *limoncello* but I gracefully refuse—it's 3 o'clock in the afternoon—and anyway, Mario, our octogenerian carpenter, has finally turned up to install the last windows and doors, and Daniele the electrician has arrived after a five month absence and there are many decisions to be made. But at least the decision about the vineyard is settled. We will level the ground in February and plant soon after, depending upon the moon. Now to choose a name for our vineyard! I am already designing bottle labels in my head.

The next morning, when I make my daily visit to Lina's house next door to chat and catch up with the village gossip, she asks, What were

Rosetta and Lina picking grapes with Ron in the middle

you doing yesterday down in the meadow with Roberta and Velia? She doesn't miss a thing. I tell her we are thinking of putting in a vineyard. Lina is a wonderful person, I just love her. But she is very attached to the old ways. She was born in Groppolo, the little hamlet above Reusa, and has lived here all her life. She says that nothing grows down in that valley because nothing CAN grow down there, it's a *pozzo*, a well. The water from the mountains and the rain storms settle there in the hollow in the clay soil and the vines will rot. They like their roots to be dry; vines need to be planted on a hillside. I listen respectfully to all that she has to say, knowing that there is much wisdom in her words. I don't tell her that we are planning to bulldoze the soil so the land is flat and that I think it will be okay to plant vines there, especially if we have the soil analyzed; I trust her instinct and her memories of the way things used to be. Then she tells me that we own land that goes up that hillside—and she waves her hand in a northwesterly direction—where we have perfectly good land for a vineyard. In fact, it was the vineyard of the previous owner of our house, and it's beautifully terraced. We have a surveyor's plan of the land that we own, but there are so many different pieces that we haven't yet figured out where it all is. So she promises to take us up the hill the next day and show us.

That evening we are invited for a farewell dinner at Velia and Roberto's as I am leaving in a few days' time, and tomorrow they have to go to Marina di Carrarra to tend to their parents' grave, for Lo It Is Written, it seems, that for *Tutti Santi*, All Saints Day on November 1st, all Italians must make a pilgrimage to the *paese*, the homeland of their parents, or grandparents, to tend their graves. And Velia and Roberto want to make sure they get there and do their duty before the rush. So we arrive for dinner, rather reluctantly because we'd already been to Spino Fiorito for our Last Lunch and we were pretty full, but how could we say NO to a promise of *polenta con fungi*, followed by *tiramisu*? So we arrive with our map of the various parcels of land in the village and show them where the old vineyard on the hillside apparently is. They are not convinced. I am worried that we have a conflict here; warring sides on where to plant the vineyard.

The next day we meet Lina without our map, because we left it at Velia's by mistake, but Lina knows exactly which is our land and which is everyone else's; she knows every inch of this village and its hillside and valleys. We skitter down the hillside on our backsides to reach the meadow and then walk up the hillside through thickets of bramble and hazel trees—our land, dreadfully, embarrassingly over-grown—to a beautiful series of terraces, hidden by the overgrowth which would make a beautiful vineyard without too much clearing. Except that Lina asks, Why do you want to have a *vigneto* anyway? It's too much work! She reckons that her son Maurizio spends so much time and money on their small vineyard that the wine costs about 100 euros a glass! She is of course exaggerating, but we get the message. She describes how the vines have to be pruned, and staked,

Ron and Riccardo decanting a demijohn of homemade wine in our cantina

and tied up, and sprayed, and if it rains twice a day, you have to go out and spray again. She tells us that her brother Amadeo had not gone out one time after it had rained—it was a very rainy summer—and his vines had become infected with *muffa,* mould. We had seen the vines in his vineyard, hanging with bunches of blackened, lifeless grapes, and knew what she meant. It was shameful. But Amadeo is 88 and can be forgiven. But could we? I begin to realize that this is a venture that we would be undertaking in full view of all our neighbors; there would be no hiding place. Our ethics towards pruning, spraying and harvesting our grapes would be pubic opinion. Could we deal with this, I am wondering? And how much can we depend on Roberto to help us?

The leaves are crisping on the trees, our neighbor Roberto's cat has taken up permanent residence on the chair in front of our kitchen fire, and many of the local residents have closed the shutters of their homes to return to the city for a few months until spring. And we will do likewise—we will leave for the US and in a few months we will come back to Italy to continue work on the downstairs part of the house, and also to work the land, the most glorious part of being in Italy—next to the people, and the food, and the wine, and the culture, and the history, and the language, challenging as it is. Italy has captured our hearts, as it has countless people before us. It's a love affair with no end in sight. And we will make a final decision about the new vineyard when we return.

Bastardo!

Tuesday, October 12, 2010

YESTERDAY, AS WE DROVE down the hill for our mid-day lunch break, the guys in good humor at the thought of a hearty meal, or more probably, a bottle of wine, we passed a tractor loaded with wood trundling up the hill. Delio learned out of the window shaking his fist and yelling good-humoredly *"Bastardo! BASTARDO!"* The others joined in: *"BASTAAARRRDO!"* It was Andrea, brother of Massimo, who had both helped us with the earth-moving when we put in the retaining walls for the terraces and swimming pool. In fact, it was Massimo who had been responsible for the collapse of the ancient wall that shelters the pool from the north. But that is another story . . .

Gabriele and Delio at lunch at Spino Fiorito

"Bastardo?" I said. I thought Andrea was a good guy. He is, he is, they said. So *"bastardo"* is good then? Yes, they said. And Massimo, is he a *bastardo* too? Yes, they yelled in unison, but he's also a *schemo* (loosely translated as an idiot). When I thought of the collapsed wall, I had to silently agree with them.

The conversation turned to Il Baffardello, the country restaurant where we had hoped to go for lunch. Being Monday, Spino Fiorito, our usual haunt, was closed. Second choice on Mondays was always Il Baffardello. But, Delio tells us, there's been a death in the family and it's closed today for the funeral. We were greatly concerned, not so much because we'd have to go to Il Re di Macchia for lunch, definitely our third choice, but because the elderly proprietor of Il Baffardello, Mario, was in the process—the long, long process—of making our windows and doors out of local chestnut wood. Maybe this would prolong the process even more? But no, as we found out— the deceased was a relative of Mario's daughter-in-law Valeria. And the restaurant was closed because she was *Il Capo*, The Boss. She was the boss because Mario's son Alberto was a *schemo*. Why is that, we asked? Because he could be helping his father run the restaurant and his carpentry business, but instead he runs around all over the place doing God knows what, with a very strong implication that other women were involved. *Que peccato* for Mario to have a son like that! they said. Alberto is definitely a b*astardo* AND a *schemo*!

Like Berlusconi, I ventured? No, they roared, Berlusconi is a *bastardo* but not a *schemo*! But he is also *furbo*, wily like a fox. Obviously one can be, and in fact probably should be, a *bastardo* to be Prime Minister, but you certainly can't be a *schemo*. But it helps to be *furbo*. In fact, it might be essential.

Living the Italian Dream

March 31, 2011

THE CHURCH BELL just clanged 4 pm and I realize I've been here for one week, exactly—we drove into Reusa as the bell struck 4 last Thursday, on a glorious sunny spring day, to find all the neighbors outside, tending their gardens or bringing in wood or just sitting and chatting. It was as if I hadn't left, everything seemed the same as it had been last October, and certainly I hadn't endured the winter they'd had here; in fact, winter on the Cape didn't seem so bad, but my memory is a bit faint by now, having settled into the Italian way of life, so that being in America seems like another lifetime. It's been a hectic week; I was thrown in at the deep end, arriving to find that the workmen had put the shower stall in wrong and it had to be torn out and redone, and making trips every day to the nearest town to pick out tiles (yet again, and I fervently hope for the last time), beds, mattresses, patio stone . . . because if they have to be ordered it can take some time, maybe weeks, and I want to see it all finished before I leave at the end of April.

Wednesday was the busiest day, everyone seemed as if by some unspoken signal to descend on Reusa on the same day—maybe they knew about the lunch special at Lo Spino?—so we had the electrician here as well as the builders, and the two guys who were putting up the *carton gesso* ceilings (sheet-rock), and Mario, our carpenter, who hadarrived unexpectedly with a gorgeous piece of aged oak two feet wide and more than two inches thick for a window sill, sadly too high up to be admired, but we know it's there and its unseen presence just adds to the beauty of the place. All the other wood is chestnut, but as the house is called Casa della Quercia, literally House of the Oak Wood, Riccardo joked that we now had a piece of genuine oak in the house! So it was a busy day and we were seven for lunch.

It's always fun having a crowd for lunch, everyone jabbering away in a mix of Italian and English, and taking their food very seriously. Tuscany ultimately is, as all who spend time here discover, about food—growing it, eating it, preparing it, discussing it.

Therefore the highlight of the working day is *pranzo*, lunch. At 10 euros per person, the *pranzo di lavoro* (workmen's lunch) is a good deal, and consists of the *primo*, first course, usually pasta or soup, followed by the *secondo*, second course, usually meat or fish with vegetables, and then *dolce*, dessert, accompanied by all the local wine you can drink. Bread and bottled water are also thrown in, as well as a shot of *limoncello* or *grappa* at the end of the meal if desired. The best lunch this week was undoubtedly on Monday at Re di Macchia in Casola (our local restaurant, Spino Fiorito, being closed that day.) The *primo* was *capra con polenta* (goat with polenta), which turned out to be a delicious casserole of goat that was so filling we didn't need a *secondo*, so the owner brought us another steaming bowl for seconds. We followed that by their specialty dessert, a chestnut pudding, the best I've ever tasted, and just about the only time I ever eat dessert! This is how the workmen eat every day; when the church bells strike noon they stop, wash up, and pile into cars to head to the restaurant of their choice.

On that very busy Wednesday, Riccardo and Davide had started at 8 am, mixing cement and preparing to lay the stones for the new outdoor patio. It was a long day, especially since Daniele, the electrician, stayed until 8 pm, trying to get as much done as he could before the light faded. We were exhausted after he left; I don't know what it is, but having all these different groups of workers asking constant questions about where does this go and how do you want that just fries my brain. Today, it was just Riccardo and Davide, so much easier to deal with. Riccardo usually has Gabriele as his sidekick, but he's working on the big project with Stefano, so his brother Davide is helping out. They work together well, Davide mixing the cement for

Riccardo, the virtuoso mason, to lay the floors and patios and build the pillars for the patio extension. They have an easy friendship and refer to each other affectionately as Riki and Dadi.

We are almost there, *quasi finito*; this project, which started nearly eight years ago, is just about finished. There is a bittersweet feeling as the end draws near, but I realize that the glamour and excitement have faded somewhat and I will be quite happy to just tend the garden and fuss about the furnishings in the future; I won't feel the urge to embark on any more major building projects. Been there, done it, and now I guess I need to make up a T-shirt that says, "Reusa: Project Completed." Today at lunch we talked about having a party on Easter Monday to celebrate the (almost) completed house. Riccardo said he thought the house would now be worth about 700,000 euros, maybe more. We are not selling, we said. Overseeing the renovation of this house, extending its life by a few centuries, has become a

View of the house, stone courtyard and outbuildings seen from the campanile (bell tower) Photo taken by Maurizio Tonelli during renovations to the campanile.

The front door of the completed house

passion. The house has been renovated with such care, such thought, such love, that the idea of selling is unimaginable. The entire experience has been extraordinary, from discovering the old ruin and then being crazy enough to take it on—to buy it, to figure out how to manage a project like this, to learn Italian, and then get to know and love our neighbors and builders and this little part of Italy. You couldn't buy this—this experience, these memories, for any amount of money. Its value to us is in the doing of it, agonizing over every decision, scraping together the money for each stage, knowing in our hearts that we would sell our souls to finish this place, and in fact, we probably did . . .

Before we started this project, we knew it would take longer and cost more than we anticipated. Were we prepared for that? We knew that we were, that this place, this beautiful, sad, neglected house, the ruin that said to us, Buy me! Love me! Save me!, had captured our hearts and we were helpless. We heeded her call, sold and mortgaged everything we could and embarked on a journey that has been life-changing. You can read as many books as you like about living *La Dolce Vita in Italia*, but it's quite another thing to actually DO it. I have to remind myself of this occasionally, when the going gets tough. Every so often, I get a glimpse of IT, that moment when I say, Yes! THIS moment, THIS view, THIS experience, THIS is why I am here, THIS is it, this is the dream, the dream I had when I was 17 and first fell in love with Italy. This is it. I am living the dream. And not a minute goes by that I am not full of gratitude for whatever had to happen to get me to this place, so many years later. It just goes to show, it's never too late. The important thing is to have the dream in the first place and then recognize it when it shows up, saying, Yes, YES, YES!

The dining arbor at Casa della Quercia

Dog Days

April 6th, 2011

TODAY STARTED like most any other day this spring: up at seven-ish, the workmen arriving around eight-ish, and after an espresso and a chat to catch up and plan the day's work, everyone was on the job by 8:30 or so. Our friend John came by to help us move some furniture into the new downstairs floor and we discovered to our dismay that the Leonardo bedroom is too small for the bed frames we'd bought, so we need to take a chunk out of the wall to get them to fit in—no problem, said Riccardo, whose motto is *tutto e possible,* everything is possible—I can do that in half a day; though, thankfully, the "antique" hand-made Italian bed frames look wonderful in the Rafaello suite—win some, lose some. I'm not too keen on the Ikea chest of drawers when I see it in situ, but old ones are hard to come by, and it'll do for now. So after the rigors of the morning's work, when the church bell struck 12 and played its little mid-day tune, we all piled into various cars and trucks for the daily ritual of lunch at Spino Fiorito. Little did we know that our lives would soon change . . .

Just about every village has a bar or restaurant that serves as its Central Intelligence Agency, a place to share information about what's going on, who's doing what, and who needs what. Ours is Spino Fiorito, an increasingly popular *agriturismo* owned by GianFranco and Gisella and their son Davide. We were truly blessed the day they opened it, about two years after we'd bought our villa. Just the other day when we were having lunch there, the postman rushed in looking for Ron, needing him to sign for his new credit card. I try to image that happening in the US. The gossip that day from the workmen who visit daily for their *pranzo di lavoro* was that renovations had

Pepe as he looked when he first arrived

been stopped on the big villa across the small valley from us, in Montonara—inspectors had visited the building site and found that most of the workers were Albanians with no papers. Someone will have to pay a large fine. The news filled the restaurant with a gleeful buzz but of course everyone was thinking, Thank Goodness it wasn't me they caught! For in Italy, everyone has something to hide.

Today as we walked towards the restaurant, we saw coming towards us in the blazing sunshine a man holding a length of white string with a lanky young dog tied to the end. "Here's your dog," explained Davide, barely able to hide his excitement. Puzzled, we looked harder at the human attached to the dog and recognized Dario, whose father owns the bar in Vigneta. Apparently Ron and his friend John had gone in there a few weeks earlier and put the word out that Ron was looking for a puppy and a kitten. Well, here was one half of that wish come true. Dario knew we would be here for lunch, so he'd brought the dog, unannounced. He said he already had several dogs and couldn't keep this one; there had been five in the litter and this was

Gillian with Pepe

the last. This sounded serious, so we took a good look at the dog in question. At five months old, Pepe seemed good natured and affectionate, with the distinctive look of a *segugio*, an Italian hunting dog, a distant relative of the bloodhound. Though most probably a mixed breed, he was an exceptionally handsome dog, with soulful eyes and a short-haired, glossy chestnut coat. Dario handed Ron the end of the string and said in Italian, He's yours. We were a bit stunned, so we turned to Riccardo to make sure we had heard right. Yes, said Riccardo, the dog is yours. What should we do? We did what all Italians would do. We took him into the restaurant with us to have lunch. Davide brought out a can of dog food which we opened at the table, and Pepe wolfed it down. Dario was sitting at a nearby table—no point in driving to Lo Spino and not having lunch there—so it was difficult for Pepe to know who to stay with, but we kept feeding him bits of chicken and he soon felt right at home under the table.

After lunch, we took Pepe back to the house and he soon settled in. As I write this, seated at a table on the *aia*, the stone patio in front of

the house, the weather is simply glorious with swallows soaring overhead and bumblebees lazily feeding at the rosemary blossoms. Pepe
is asleep on a quilt at my feet and seems very happy to be here—at
least, happy not to be competing with five other dogs for food and
affection. As far as we are concerned, he is here to stay, and he seems
to feel the same way. And so it goes, life in a small Italian village. It
makes the Real World seem so far away.

Not All Fun & Games in Italy
or the further adventures of Life with a Landie

October 2011

YOU WOULD HAVE THOUGHT a routine trip to Pisa airport in the Land Rover, which we've done many, many times, would be business as usual. Unfortunately, not so. As we were taking my daughter Tessa and Ryan, her boyfriend at the time, back to the airport after a 10 day vacation, the Landie stalled on the autostrada just outside Viareggio, about 20 minutes from the airport, and 20 minutes before they were due to check in. After the engine cut out, we cruised gently into an emergency lay by, mostly used as an outdoor toilet by the look of things. The one thing that "austerity" had meant in Italy, it appears, is that the roadside verges are no longer cut, with sprouting weeds and brambles that just about fill up the width of country lanes, and garbage pick-up has largely been eliminated. Litter floats freely from where it is jettisoned from passing cars and unfortunately, at least down on the plain where we now were, it's an eyesore.

What to do? We hailed another truck at the lay by who directed us to the phone booth especially placed there for events of this sort. Choosing the *mecanico* button, signified by a picture of a blue wrench, I was able to make someone on the other end understand that we'd broken down at the first exit after Camaoire, as the truck driver was so helpful to tell me. I'll be there in 20 minutes, said the voice on the other end of the phone. It was hard to believe this might be possible, but since the kids HAD to get on that plane back to the US and back to work, it was our only hope. About 15 minutes later we saw the flashing lights of a tow truck arriving. The driver called a taxi, and we all clambered into the cab while we watched the Landie being hauled up onto a towing vehicle and carted off to a garage somewhere in Viareggio. This was a sensitive moment. The Landie had taken us all over Italy, across France, down through Spain, and all through Morocco with never a hiccup, except when Ron took a bend on the Tiz and Tes pass in the atlas Mountains, met a bus coming the other way and veered too close to the side of the road, hitting the branch of a tree. The branch clipped the side of the windshield and I, in the passenger seat, watched as 13 cracks appeared as if in slow-motion, starting from the right hand side, as you look out, and ending up somewhere in the middle, so the driver had a clear vision, but the passenger, and, more importantly, the navigator—me—had a very fractured view. But it was better than shattering the windshield entirely.

We may have complained that the Landie was too wide for Italy's country lanes, or sounded like a tractor due to its diesel engine, or that the roof leaked after a heavy rain, but in fact it had given us seven years of impeccable service. It was sad to see her being born away on a towing vehicle. We wished her well and sped off to the airport, our only concern being that we got the kids on that plane.

Thankfully, we reached the airport just in time to get them checked in. But the line for security stretched from one end of the airport to the other—and that's a long line, now that Pisa airport has recently doubled in size. Ron did his usual thing of telling some tall tale about why they had to get to the front of the line and we hugged them goodbye as they entered the winding lanes that fed into the scanning machines. Somewhat satisfied with ourselves, we treated ourselves to a *pannino* (sandwich) and a *caffé macchiato*—is Pisa the only international airport in the world that has an outdoor café?—and strolled over to the adjacent train station to catch a train to Viareggio to reclaim our vehicle.

We called the garage that had towed the vehicle when we reached

Viareggio and they told us it could not be fixed that day, but surely would be fixed by the next. So we had to rent a car to drive us home and back there the next day. But of course it was *ora di pranzo*, lunch time, and the only car rental in town, EuropCar, was closed until 3 pm. So we walked down to the beach to catch some sea air and by the time we got back they had opened up. Renting the car and driving back home was the easiest part of the previous couple of days. The day before, we had finally got all the paperwork together, and the required personnel, to close on the purchase of our neighbor Roberto's barn and the various bits of land that we had needed to join up our own pieces so we could build the swimming pool on contiguous land. This we had done five years previously, but with the *geometra* taking so long to make up the plans showing the sub-division, and then us not having enough cash on hand to pay the exorbitant tax that the government requires when a foreigner buys property, we had put the closing off for as long as possible. But the sellers, our neighbors Lina and her sons Maurizio and Doriano, could wait no longer, as Doriano had cancer which was progressing rapidly. When I saw him at the lawyer's office I was horrified and saddened, and knew what it meant—that it was the last time I'd see him, this sweet and gentle person. Maurizio explained that since he and his brother had inherited the property from their father, if Doriano died before we completed the sale, it would complicate the whole deal.

So we met at the *notaio*'s office at the appointed time, Ron and I, Lina and her two sons, Karsten the interpreter, Vittorio the geometra, and the *notaio* himself, very slick in his hand-tailored suit, Gucci shoes and oiled hair, a handsome and distinguished man probably in his early 60s, and his assistant. The process was tortuous, more concerned about the anti-maffia laws than about whether we were actually purchasing the various numbered pieces of land we had been promised in the *promesso*. We all gave our passports to be copied and recorded, our *codice fiscale* numbers, and all the documents, and Vittorio handed over the plans—all for a barn and a few bits of land!

But in Italy anything that involves the exchange of money or property is taken extremely seriously. The *notaio* started to read out the document that we all had to sign: everyone's names, everyone's ages, everyone's correct address, and everyone's marital status. The notaio rattled through this until he got to one Drake, Gillian Herbert . . . *Sei sposata?* He looked at me (Are you married?) I said, No. He stopped the proceedings, took off his glasses and stared harder. *Sei sola?* he asked me (Are you single?) Yes, I said. He took another hard look followed by a long pause and then said, with great feeling, *Een-cre-dee-bee-lay*! (Incredible), shook his head, and continued rattling on with the reading of the document. I didn't know whether to be ashamed or flattered, but Lina said something encouraging, I'm not quite sure what, and we all continued.

After some heart-stopping moments over the fact that the checks we had written over the years to pay for the barn might not be acceptable because they might have been considered to be transferable, which is not allowed since the new anti-mafia law was introduced in 2005 and which incurs a fine of many, many thousands of euros, we were so relieved when it was all over that we stumbled out into the dusk and headed straight for the nearest bar. So we already were a bit stressed out before the incident with the Landie.

The next day we left the dog in the house and headed down to Viareggio in our little rented Fiat 500, zipping along the autostrada to retrieve the Landie. After a quick lunch we went to the car rental place to return the car to find they were still closed—for lunch!— and would not open until 3 pm. We waited patiently to give them back the car, and then hired a cab to take us to the auto repair shop, praying that the Land Rover would be ready. It was—and the bill was close to 1300 euro. That's outrageous, we said! You took seven hours to install a new fuel pump? said Ron, shaking his head in amazement. When the garage owner didn't budge, Ron called his bluff, saying, You can have the vehicle, it's not even worth that. The garage owner shrugged; he really didn't want a 1998 Land Rover. But we have learned to not take these Italian banditos lying down. When all else fails, a hissy fit in English tames the most resolute Italian, but we went one better—we called Maurizio, Lina's son and our neighbor, who just happened to be the tax collector for our *comune* of Casola. He shamed the garage owner and got the price down to 1,000 cash. But we didn't have cash. Ah! But we could write a check. There was actually no money in the account, but he didn't know that, so we wrote a check and drove off in haste, intent on getting back home as soon as possible to let our dog Pepe out of the house. No such luck. As we navigated around Aulla and set off on the by-pass near the new railway station on the last leg of our journey home, the fuel pump cut out again and the vehicle stopped dead in its tracks. We were stunned. We had just paid 1,000 euros to get her going.

Long story short, after more expensive adventures closer to home and the help of a couple of complete strangers, we finally got back— somehow—to our house. What a relief to be HOME! I felt like Mole in "Wind in the Willows" getting back to his burrow after his adventures in the Wild Wood.

After recovering from our adventure, we asked around and sold the Land Rover to the first person to come up with 1,000 euros. We still see her chugging around the locality with a load of hunting dogs and guns in the back, like a kind of Italian shooting brake. We are glad she still has a bit of life left in her, but we are now looking for a more sensible car, something narrow enough to navigate the country lanes, and is reliable—or at least, won't cost an arm and a leg if it breaks down inconveniently, or, preferably, one that doesn't break down at all.

Roberto (il scultore) and Ida

October 22nd, 2012

THE FIRST LIGHT woke me this morning, just as the mist was lifting from the valley and just before the sun rose above the mountains. The owls were making their last calls, and the blackbirds were singing in the olive trees as if it were spring, not the middle of autumn. As I was becoming fully awake, I heard a strange rushing sound, as though a water pipe had burst outside. I got out of bed and opened the window that looked out over the valley and saw the line of trees below swaying and bending under a squall of wind, invisible except for its effects. The roar continued as the wind stormed through the valley, sending showers of bright gold leaves into the airs, swirling around and around, and then passed on up the hills to the mountain, and calm descended once again. A minute later, the same thing happened, another puff of wind scurried up the valley, disturbing all in its path.

Soon after, as I was walking down the hill towards Roberto's (Roberto the Sculptor) house to get a dozen fresh eggs, I passed Lida tending her zucchini bush, which is now more like a tree, trained on a stake at least 5 ft high. *Buon giorno*, I said jovially, what a wind! It's beginning to feel like autumn! She looked at me and said, more like winter. And then I saw she was wearing her quilted down jacket. What wimps they are here, I thought, always expecting perfect weather—any weather that isn't perfect is *brutto*, horrible. Obviously they've never lived in England, or New England, both home to really *brutto* tempo, foul weather, at times—and in fact, a lot of the time. But here in Italy, I am grateful for each and every day, no matter the weather . . .

As Pepe and I walked down the hill, I saw Roberto in the road outside his house, picking up the last of the chestnuts. Not many this year, he remarked; there's an insect that's attacking the trees, and they are dying—the effects of global warming. Everyone is very depressed about it, as we are surrounded by chestnut trees, it's our landscape, and if they all died, the landscape would be bare. In fact, chestnuts used to be a staple food around here, and there's a chestnut festival in Regnano on Saturday, where we can sample the traditional foods that were made from chestnuts—breads and cakes and pancakes and desserts.

Roberto led me through the gates into his garden, chock full of fruit trees and berry bushes, round to the main entrance in the back. I left Pepe in the front hall where Roberto does his wood carving, and entered the kitchen to chat with Ida, his wife. She had grown up here, in Reusa; she was born during the war and remembers those days. Her mother had died when she was five, of fright, she says, after years of Nazi occupation. I didn't want to ask for details. She had been born in the old house next door, but she and her husband had built this new house, and now the old one lay rotting and abandoned. She is always happy for company, so I sat at the table with her. There's always a lot to chat about, though often I can't remember afterwards precisely what it was we chatted about. But sometimes I do arrive home with a nugget of precious information—something that is the missing piece to a puzzle that we'd not quite understood about our little community, or some gossip about a neighbor.

I remember I told them that we had just been to meet Alessandra in Casola who we hope will be caring for Pepe while we are away this winter. Casola! Exclaimed Roberto! Do you think he'll stay there? We all laughed—Pepe is known to wander. One day Roberto had seen him strolling down the main street of Casola, and had called Ron to let him know so he could drive over to pick him up. But we agreed that Pepe is a bit older now and not so prone to wander. Anyway, if he does take off, he's close to home—Casola is only a few miles from Reusa, and all our neighbors know him, so if they see him, they'll call up Alessandra, since her phone number will be on his dog collar.

Roberto, too, will look out for Pepe, we know that—he's a dog lover. He and another neighbor Rosetta are caring for two dogs that were abandoned on our country road about a year ago and were living in the woods. Rosetta found a place for them in her barn, and she feeds them every morning, walking the mile or so down the hill with a bag of food, and Roberto feeds them in the evening. They are hoping, he said, to get some English people in a neighboring village to help with the feeding, or even adopt them, as the English are known to be great dog lovers. The dogs are very sweet, one black, one dappled, little hounds the size of beagles. Of course they are timid around strangers, but would be very nice companion dogs for someone who wanted one. Sadly, no one seems to want them yet.

Roberto and Ida at Davide and Gabriella's wedding with Lina in the background

I chatted some more with Ida while Roberto went to get the eggs. I offered a 10 euro note to pay for the eggs, but she refused. I told her that I can't keep coming here for eggs if she won't let me pay for them! She said they were a gift since we had made Reusa—her home village, her *paese*—so beautiful. I reflected on the huge amount of time, effort and, yes, money, that we had spent on our house, and I had to agree with her. The village had looked pretty much derelict before we renovated that house, which takes up at least a third of the real estate of the *antico borgo*, the medieval village center. And Roberto, who had just arrived with a huge carrier bag full of apples from his trees, added, The hens have laid them anyway! We can't eat them all!

It seems they supply the whole village with eggs, just as Mario does with his tomatoes and Angelo with his kiwi fruit at Christmas. The only person who doesn't seem to share is Sebastiano, with his huge *orto* down in the valley—we have never been offered anything by Sebastiano, and neither has anyone else, as far as I know. I wonder where it all goes. Maybe he sells it? He used to be in finance before he retired, at the port of Genoa—maybe, being money-oriented, he sells his produce to supplement his retirement income.

Ida continued to chat and her Italian drifted over me like a snowy blanket, and it didn't seem to matter that I only understood about half of what she was saying. My attention was caught by her goldfish who had a kind of cyst on its belly so it floated around the tank upside down, a bizarre sight. I refocused and joined in the conversation. She was telling me how she was allergic to so many things, including perfume and various chemical smells. I said I was sensitive, *sensitivo*, too. She said, no, you are *sensible, sensitivo* means you are psychic. So I said, I am that too! And she said, so am I! And told me about a time when she was at college near Genoa and saw a nun float down some steps and disappear through a wall. I tried to tell her that my gift was different, I knew things without knowing how I knew them, but my

Italian failed me—or maybe it was lack of her comprehension. Anyway, we are now firm friends, being both *sensible*.

I thanked them both and took Pepe by the leash, and we struggled up the hill laden with eggs and apples, probably the last of this year's harvest. All the walnuts are now down from the trees, the chestnuts too, and the last of the figs are green and hard on the bare twigs. It's time to put the garden away until next spring. Next spring. What a joyful thought. If ever I need to lift my spirits, I remind myself that there will always be another spring in Italy.

View from the villa, spring 2014

Monday Always Starts Slow

April 2, 2012

MONDAYS ALWAYS START SLOWLY, a result of the exertions of
the day before, Sunday, when Italians put a lot of effort into taking
it easy—which can include driving long distances to visit family or
a country restaurant for a special lunch that can take four hours to
complete. But this Sunday, the special attraction was the *Fiera del
Cucu* (Feast of the Cuckoo) in our local town of Casola, which takes
place each year on the first Sunday of April—and which this year
happened to fall on the first of the month. In England, there's a tradition that the cuckoo arrives on April 1st; country folk have devel-
oped a habit of writing to *The Times* announcing the date and time
they hear the first cuckoo if it's before the magical date of April 1st;
after that, it's not news.

April 1st in Italy can be rainy and chilly, but yesterday, the sun shone
in a continuation of an early spring heat wave. The narrow stone-
flagged lanes of Casola were swept clean of debris and stray cats and
lined with tables and demonstrations of traditional crafts such as
spinning and weaving and pottery making, while the main street,
closed to through traffic, was filled with commercial stalls selling
everything from clothes, toys, cut flowers and garden plants to local
produce, wine, cheese, and just about anything an Italian house-wife
or *contadino* might need. Center stage was a large refrigerated van
which provided fair-goers with *pannini* (sandwiches) stuffed with
slices carved from a whole roasted pig. A few of the basements of
the town's narrow stone houses had been turned into rudimentary
kitchens where volunteers in a rather haphazard way prepared food
for passersby—traditional delicacies such as *cian*, a chestnut pan-

cake stuffed with *ricotta,* and *sgabai,* a kind of sandwich stuffed with *pancetta* and cream cheese, fried in olive oil and rolled in salt—and dispensed plastic beakers of local wine, all in aid of Bosnian orphans.

Members of the local historical association strutted about in medieval costumes, and for a moment the town looked as it must have done hundreds of years before. To me, the most interesting part of this historical display was a table laid out with swatches of linen dyed by traditional methods. I was transfixed by the realization that in past centuries, the world would have looked different. There would have been no harsh chemical dyes, only these that I saw in front of me—pale yellow from saffron, a golden yellow from turmeric, a delicate lavender from myrtle berries, an orangey tint from onion skins, a soft brown from walnuts, and many more. The dyes weren't fast so they would have faded with wear and washing, and what a picture it must have been, to see everyone dressed in home-spun clothes dyed in these soft shades, what harmony the colors must have created.

And that brings me to the subject of paint colors. The wonderful faded facades of Tuscan buildings, much copied the world over, seem to be fading into memory, or, worse, painted over. The old lime paints have been replaced with garish acrylic colors, not so obvious when the chosen color is cream or pale pink, but a disaster with stronger shades, such as terra cotta, which can appear as burnt orange in full sunlight, or lemon yellow looking like egg-yolk. Our neighbor Lina has had the stucco of her house newly painted a delicate shade of knicker-pink, not too bad by itself, but the Bacci family above chose to paint their house a vivid shade of orange, not a good match in full sunlight, and it shines like a beacon when viewed across the valley. I am determined to buy old-fashioned lime paint to touch up the stubborn bits of concrete that we can't chip off the old stone walls—that way the color will fade in the time-honored Tuscan way.

The best thing about the *fiera* was that the museum in Casola was open for the day. We have been here for nine years and never had been able to visit the museum. When a law was passed that all public buildings must have a handicapped entrance, the town couldn't afford to put in a lift, so the museum has been closed ever since. But today it was staffed by volunteers and we gladly paid our three euro so we could wander through the old palazzo, looking at copies of stone-age *steli* statues (the carved originals are in the museum in Pontremoli), and medieval tools. But what caught my eye was a map showing the *Francigena*, the ancient Pilgrim's Way, that followed a path from Canterbury, in England, though France and Switzerland to the holy city of Rome, and then across Italy to the southern port of Brindisi where the pilgrims could take a boat to Jerusalem. Having just witnessed the *antico borgo* filled with medieval-looking folk, my mind was in the past and I absorbed this information with a deeper understanding of this undertaking. These pilgrims walked from England to Rome with nothing but the clothes on their back, living off the kindness of strangers and the beneficence of the Church—what an incredible adventure of faith and fortitude that must have been.

Looking closely at the map showing the pathways that spread like a spider's web across Europe, to Lourdes and Campostella de Santiago in the west and down to Rome in the south, I saw that the leg from Pontremoli to Lucca, called the Via del Volto Santo, went right through our village of Reusa. Not only that, it went through our property. Not only that, it went through our HOUSE. And it hit me with a flash: our house, or rather, the group of ancient buildings that make up our house, was probably at one time a boarding house for pilgrims. I knew it had never been a farmhouse, like most of the larger buildings in these parts, and it couldn't have been built as priests' quarters, since there's no sign of a monastery having ever been here. But with the Roman road running alongside our house and its guard post situated under our front patio, this was obviously an important stop along the way to Lucca. The whole idea totally captivated me, and ever since I have been researching the routes of the old pilgrims' ways and imagining buying and converting Lina's magnificent house next door into a bed-and-breakfast for modern-day pilgrims hiking the old route, which the province of Tuscany is now promoting . . . Well, it's good to dream!

Monday may have started slowly, but after a leisurely morning recovering from Sunday's exertions, our tranquility was interrupted when I noticed a familiar white truck driving up the hill towards our house. Could it be . . .? I called to Ron, " I think it's Mario!" Ron, who was enjoying a short nap on the couch with Pepe, leapt up and was as shocked as I was to see Mario, our carpenter, clamber out of the truck in his uniform of faded blue overalls. He hadn't been seen since last October, which was strange, because the job he'd been working on hadn't been quite finished and we thought we might still owe him some money. We didn't know if he'd become a bit forgetful (he is over 80), or had got bored with the job, or just couldn't deal with Ron's rudimentary Italian . . . but it turned out that in fact he had lost his driving license. In Italy, in an effort to control the insane driving habits that would make a Boston driver blanche, there is now a system where each infraction counts as points, and after 20 points, you lose your license. And when you lose your license, you have to take your driving test again! It had taken Mario five months and over a thousand euros to do all the paper work and testing to get his driver's license back. And that's why we hadn't seen him for so long. He admitted he'd been stopped by the police twice, but reassured us that his eyesight is fine, so he shouldn't get stopped again, but we knew it wasn't as issue with his eyesight, it was more about drinking too much wine. A man is dead without his driver's license, he told us several times. Yes, very true, especially in these remote mountain villages, when he would have no way to get around to visit his clients. One of the reasons he'd come to see us was that Riccardo our builder had got in touch with him as we needed to have a window measured for the little chestnut drying house we are turning into a sixth bedroom. He measured the window, a bit confused at first by our tape measure that was marked in inches, and then casually asked, Did we have any money for him?—obviously the second reason for his visit. Our hearts stopped. This seems to happen a lot. As most of the commerce in Italy goes on "under the table," because the VAT tax is now a whopping 21 percent, nothing is written down, so it's very easy to lose track. We don't have written estimates from the electrician or the plumber either for the work on the downstairs floor, and we really have no more than a vague idea what the job has cost and how much more we owe.

We asked Mario how much he thought we owed him . . . five hundred euro maybe? No, he said, more like four or five thousand. In the heat of the moment, I am trying to figure out the difference between *cinquecento* (500) and *cinquemila* (5,000). But five THOUSAND is a lot different from five hundred! We gulped and said we'd come to see him the next evening and go over the work he'd done (a couple of doors and a window) and try and figure out how much we owed him. It can't be more than three thousand, we think to ourselves. Everything is negotiable, especially when cash is involved. Maybe we can get him to come down a bit. Yes, he said, come to my workshop and we'll share a beer. We'll do that tomorrow. After having got the main part of the business out of the way, he launched into a glowing review of the work that we (including him!) had done on this old house, how everyone is talking about it. They say, "Have you seen the house in Reusa?" He waggles the fingers of his right hand at the end of a straight arm, aimed towards his body, and makes a kind of *boh!* sound through his teeth (what's left of them) in that way the Italians have. The workmanship, the attention to detail, the historical stonework, the harmony! What perfection! Then he tells us about another house that he's making the windows for where he feels there is too much wood. Wood everywhere! he says with a sigh. I try to formulate a sentence in Italian outlining the important points of Feng Shui, but realize that's a stretch. Enough to say that it's good to have a balance between stone, iron, wood and clay, that it creates harmony. He understands and agrees. *Harmonia!* So important. We all feel very pleased with ourselves for having been a part of creating this truly special house, forgetting for a moment that it's taken nine years and we dare not even attempt to add up the final cost . . . best to call it "a labor of love" and leave it at that.

As Mario drives away, our neighbor's son Maurizio arrives with a clutch of cousins from Genoa here to visit his mother, Lina. She was recently bereaved when her oldest son Doriano, Maurizio's brother, died just two months before at the age of 59. "My life is not worth living now," she says. "It's over for me. I expected to mourn my parents, my dead husband, even my beloved younger sister, but I never thought I'd spend my last years mourning the death of my first born!" We all try and comfort her, but every day she cries, tears pouring down her cheeks. *Era cosi dolce!* she wails. "He was so sweet." But the worst part was that he worked for 35 years and only collected his pension for one month! How unfair that seems. I remind her she has another son to love and care about, but she spits out, *"Boh!"* and explains that he never stops for more than a few moments; he has three jobs and runs around all the time, here, there, zoom, zoom, never stopping, there's never time to talk. I think about how Maurizio comes to see her every day, is the one who fixes all her plumbing problems and roof leaks, takes care of the land, cuts the grass, makes the wine, collects the olives, chops firewood cut from their land higher up the mountain and brings it down in a tractor for her to heat her house in the winter, while Doriano, who lived in the city of La Spezia, about an hour away, would visit once or twice a month, and always had a severe back problem that needed heavy medication. But apparently, he was the favored son. We all miss Doriano, he was the sweetest person, just as she said, and we hope her mood will lighten as Easter approaches. Lent is a mournful time to be missing someone you love so much.

Maurizio takes this opportunity to tell us that Pepe, our Italian hunting dog, was seen chasing a young deer through the woods that morning, and he reminds us that we have to keep him in for the first two weeks in May when the fawns are born. That's going to be difficult for a country dog used to going where and when he pleases and who is having a hard time learning English! He doesn't seem to heed *"vieni qua!"* much either, Italian for "come here." But he is a wonderful dog, we really were so lucky.

We spent the rest of the afternoon working in the garden, trimming lavender and weeding, getting ready to plant geraniums for our summer rental season. The cold snap in February has finished off a few creeping rosemary plants, and some of the lavender bushes are getting woody, so we need to buy more. And another couple of cypress trees would be nice. Our Italian neighbors don't like them, they think they belong in cemeteries, but I love the classic look of tall dark green cypresses punctuating the landscape. The wisteria is about to burst into bloom, such a glorious sight, but it seems such a shame that it happens when none of our guests are here to see it. Wild honeybees are buzzing around feeding off the rosemary blossoms and it seems like all is right with the world. Except for the anxiety of knowing that we owed unspecified amounts of money to certain contractors! Then, just as the sun slipped behind the mountain at six and I started to put away my gardening tools, I heard my first cuckoo, only one day late. I looked up towards the place where the sound was coming from and saw that the entire valley was full of thistle down floating gently about, here and there, suddenly visible due to the angle of the sunlight. It was a magical sight.

Soon after, Rolf's friend Martin arrived with his wife and three young children after a 16-hour drive from Aachen in Germany in a mini-van towing a trailer. Last December they had bought a piece of land, an overgrown olive grove and an old stone ruin, across the little valley from us in Montenara where they had positioned their small caravan. Their caravan had been on Rolf's property for the past ten years, but Rolf (from Germany) sold his house last summer to Xavier (from Belgium, the EU ambassador to Ethiopia) who had recently purchased the large villa next door. His villa had no land so he was glad to buy it, and Rolf was glad to sell, since his two little children are growing fast and he needed the money to buy a house in Germany. He'd bought the barn when he had been a student in Italy 20 years earlier for just a few thousand euros, and was able to sell for a huge profit. We were glad for him, but it was a concern since Ron had lived in Rolf's little barn the previous summer while our villa was rented in return for doing some plastering and plumbing. Where would Ron and Pepe go this summer? Happily, Xavier offered his half-renovated villa to Ron for the summer. Problem solved.

Over the years of visiting their friend Rolf, Martin and his family had grown to love this area so much that they bought the aforementioned land and moved the caravan there. But we had noticed that the cara-

View of Quercia taken from Groppolo, two of the five hamlets that make up the village of Reusa

van was tilted at a 20 degree angle and it didn't look like it would be too comfortable to live in, and, this being April, the weather was a bit damp and still chilly at night. As it was their first trip to their new home, we took pity on them and insisted they stay in our downstairs apartment. Then we realized they must be hungry and tired after the long drive so we invited them to dinner. They gladly accepted, and so soon after we found ourselves on the mountain road heading towards Fivizzano to buy groceries for dinner. Later that evening we were enjoying a convivial meal of pasta with pesto and chicken casserole with olives, followed by *biscotti* (known as *cantucci* in our area) dipped in *vin santo*, a kind of fortified wine, and getting to know our new neighbors in a mix of German, Italian and English. We listened to Martin's plans for clearing the land and eventually building a house on the footprint of the old ruin, a place where he and his three children could come to escape the pressures and climate of Northern Europe. We remembered our enthusiasm when we bought our own ruin nine years ago and the vision that kept us going throughout the renovations, not to mention the utter ignorance of the cost and the problems we'd run into, and the blind faith that someone, somewhere, somehow would be able to put this huge pile of stones into some kind of order. That turned out to be Riccardo, Stefano and the gang. Thanks to them, it's just about finished now. We always say that, but there's always something else to do—only one more barn to renovate and then we are done! But we already have our eye on another house, one that's crying out for renovation. "Help me, Save me, Love me," it sings, flaunting its ancient stone walls and musty wine cellars, a familiar siren song tempting us with a new project. Can we resist? Only time will tell.

The Real Italy

A Visit to the Dentist and the Vet

THERE COMES A TIME, as most people who have two homes find out, when you have to choose whether you are "on vacation" or actually living there. Where to file taxes? Sign up for medical care? Visit the dentist? And so on.

I decided the time had come to try an Italian dentist. My trusted dentist on the Cape had retired, about the same time as my optometrist and accountant—all members of the baby-boomer generation, like me, doing the unthinkable, realizing that it was time to take a break from the daily grind, aka retiring. I had gone to see the new dentist who had taken over the practice and was dismayed when he had pointed out some faint shadows on my x-rays and suggested I might have some tooth decay in those teeth, and that could not be refilled—the fillings were too large. Therefore—drum roll—those three teeth would need to be crowned. I know what that would cost and gulped. But in examining the film, I failed to see, or even sense, that there was anything sinister going on in my mouth. It seemed like a lot of dental work to have done when I wasn't sure of the urgency and need. In short, I didn't have any concrete evidence. So I asked for copies of my x-rays and took them to Italy with me, and that is how I found myself in Francesco's dental studio in Santa Stefano di Magra.

Riccardo had suggested this dentist. His wife's friend Monica, who helps clean our villa on Saturdays in the summer, had been one of his dental hygienists for many years and highly recommended him. Riccardo was in the middle of a major reconstruction project himself—six implants and about 18,000 euros worth of work. I shuddered to think of the cost of that in the US. For that was my major motivation in coming here: the three crowns that my dentist in the US said I needed to have would cost 1800 each, for a shocking total of $5,400, whereas in Italy, a crown costs about 500 euros, about $650, for a total of about $2,000, a huge difference.

Francesco told Riccardo that the three of us should turn up at 6 pm next Monday evening. I am used to the American way of setting up individual appointments, but in Italy, it seems, everyone turns up at opening time and waits. No one, even successful dentists, seem to have a receptionist. So we dutifully showed up at 6 pm, Riccardo, Ron and me, only to find the tiny waiting room already full of patients. But after a short wait, we were greeted warmly by Francesco himself, a dashing figure—young, tall, slim, and heart-throb handsome in his blue combat suit, the George Clooney of Massa-Carrarra. He had paused in his frenetic dashing from one exam room to the next, his finger in every pie, or mouth, greeting everyone with a slap on the back, or a joke, staring intently into open mouths. He reminded me of a juggler, keeping ten plates spinning in the air all at once. He was full of energy, a bright spark, obviously in love with what he did—he was indeed a star. He ushered all three of us into an examining room where he checked Riccardo's progress—with us in the room. That seemed unusual; was that being friendly, informal, or . . . well, not very professional? But this is Italy, where communication, friendliness and openness are everything.

When Francesco had dismissed Riccardo, he went off with Ron to get pizza, as it was obvious there was no time for him to clean Ron's teeth that evening. He whisked me into a dental chair and loaded the zip drive into his computer and perused my x-rays. He looked at my teeth, tapped them—any pain, he asked? No, no pain, I said. There's nothing wrong with them, he pronounced, and proceeded to clean my teeth himself with some kind of high tech water pick. Every so often his cell phone would ring. One thing to know about Italians is that they will never, ever not answer their cell phone. So there I was, with various metallic instruments dangling out of my mouth, and Francesco answering the phone every few minutes. After about 15 minutes of this, he pronounced me done and sent me home. He didn't know my full name, I hadn't signed any forms, and I hadn't paid. Ron was to come back the next Monday, so I guess we'd get a bill then. I thought the cleaning a bit cursory, but in fact, my teeth had never felt cleaner. And I certainly felt relieved, knowing I didn't have to look forward to a major dental project and the cost that would entail—either in euros or in US dollars.

We had a similar experience yesterday when our dog Pepe had a cyst on his side that was growing larger every day and we decided we needed to take him to the vet. We drove him to the veterinarian's clinic over the mountain in Posaro in our little Punto, taking the back roads, aware of the new law that says we can only transport a dog in a car if we have a net that stretches across the width of the car behind the front seats. We didn't have one. Pepe rarely goes in the car so we hadn't bothered to get one; another thing to add to the list of THINGS TO GET.

Vittorio's surgery opens at four, *dopo pranzo*, after lunch. In Italy, not much happens between noon and 3; most shops and offices close for lunch until 3:30, or 4 pm, but they do stay open late, around 7 or 7:30. We arrived at 3:30, hoping to get ahead of the queue, but there were already two people waiting. Again, no appointments; you turn up and wait. So we waited. And waited. I counted the hooks on the vaulted ceiling, 16 of them. Obviously, this had once been the *cantina* of the old villa, and those were the hooks on which had hung haunches of pork, being gently cured by the smoke from the fire to become *prosciutto*. The old cellar still had that musty smell of damp flagstones, with the faint aroma of well-ripened goat's cheese and a hint of furniture polish. It was furnished with two ancient wooden wardrobes in each of the archways set into the walls, and an old oak dining table with half a dozen chairs around it sat in the center of the room, covered in leaflets. I gathered up the leaflets, shuffled them into order, and stacked them in neat piles. I read every poster on the walls. I studied the photo of Vittorio as a young man delivering a horse of a black foal. I took Pepe for walk around the block, up the hill, and down to the river. And then came back and sat and waited some more.

Finally, the vet appeared after spending about an hour with the dog before us. He was sucking down the fumes of a newly-lit cigarette, his reward for saving another dog's life. Like Francesco, he was full of energy, joking with everyone, calling the pets by name, referring to ours as Ciccio although he was called Pepe. It had been a while since he neutered him, nearly four years earlier. He jovially invited us into his office and examined Pepe; he has to have this cyst lanced, he told us, and he'd need to be sedated. I looked around the surgery. It was in the old kitchen of the villa, the bread oven was behind his desk serving as a kind of filing cabinet. In a small room next door, a large dog lay very still on an operating table. He's in a coma, Vittorio explained. What's that in English? he said. Oh yes, coma. What from? we asked. A viper's bite, he answered. Will he be okay? we asked. Oh yes, he'll be up and walking by Sunday. Today was Wednesday, that's a long time. He gave him a drink of water from a plastic syringe. He'd be doing that every couple of hours until the dog could lap water by himself—he had no assistant, it was all up to him. We were relieved to hear this story, as there's some hysteria about vipers here—though you hardly ever see them, as they are quite rare and easily scared away, but they are very dangerous. It's said you need to get to a hospital immediately, if you are bitten by one. If that dog survived a viper's bite, then there's a good chance a human can, too.

But it meant that Pepe could not be tended to in the operating room, so we had to get him up on the examining table, as that would serve as the operating table. Ron and Vittorio lifted him up, and then Vittorio reminded Ron that he'd passed out the last time he was there, and advised him to leave the room. That left me holding Pepe while Vittorio gave him a sedative and started to shave the area where he'd make the incision. I suddenly realized that I was the vet's assistant. I held Pepe's head as best I could but he jerked his head around as the vet made a small incision, and we realized he needed a general anesthetic. Vittorio deftly inserted a line into a vein in one of his front legs and hooked up a drip for the anesthetic. But still Pepe reacted—he is a strong hunting dog, he wasn't going to go under with just one vial of anesthetic! So the vet administered another, and finally Pepe lay his head down and relaxed.

Then, oddly, I heard the first few bars of Ave Maria ring out, and realized it was Vittorio's cell phone. That was to happen several times during the operation, and each time, no matter what he was doing, he answered it. Eventually, and thankfully, he sent me out of the office, saying he could manage the rest on his own. I was feeling a

bit shaky, mainly from trying to calm Pepe, and it was a relief to sit down.

A young woman was waiting with her cat in a crate, she'd been there at least two hours, and a young family had come in with their son and his puppy, not more than 8 weeks old, a cute furry little bundle with a curly tail. The door to the waiting room had been left open and we could see that the warm, sunny afternoon was fading and slowly turning to dusk. We hoped Pepe was doing okay.

As we sat there wondering, the vet opened the door and invited us in. He lit his habitual post-operative cigarette and waved his hand towards the prone dog, telling us that all went well. He administered a small shot of antidote and told us that Pepe would wake up in three minutes, as if he were a magician. And in fact, as if by magic, he lifted his head in three minutes' time. His wound was oozing so we asked for a bandage so he wouldn't bleed all over the car, and Vittorio grabbed a square of gauze and carefully squeezed out a line of Bostick glue around the edges of the gauze, and stuck the patch on Pepe's flank. I guess 30 years of experience had taught him the most effective solution.

I looked around the room at the desk covered in papers, the counter top crammed higgledy-piggledy with glass jars, vials and instruments. This vet was obviously a one-man band—no assistant, no receptionist, no bookkeeper. He sat down at his computer and printed out a bill for us: 80 euros, and 20 percent tacked on as tax for the Italian government. By this time, Pepe was able to walk, so we led him out into the car to start his two-week convalescence. After profuse thanks to Vittorio, and apologies to those still waiting for taking so long, we said our good byes and joined Pepe in the car. And I'm thinking as we drove away, that would have cost us more than $1,000 in the US. I add that to my potential US dental bill, and realize I've saved enough money for us to have one heck of a winter vacation.

Farewell Amadeo

YESTERDAY, THE BELL TOLLED for Amadeo, Lina's brother, and today we buried him. Well, not exactly, he and his coffin were slid gently into a shelf in a wall in the little village cemetery down the hill from the church, since the churchyard has long since filled up.

Because our village church was damaged in the earthquake, we could not have the church service at our local church but instead it was held at the nearby village of Codiponte, once, many centuries ago, a Roman place of worship with very graphic pagans designs on the pillars inside. Our neighbor Angelo had told us that he'd passed on at 5 am on the morning of the previous day, hailing us down as we drove into Fivizzano. Details like that are important here. Yesterday, the village was unusually quiet until the bell tolled—the bass bell tolling away mournfully, ending with a couple of ding-dongs as the three

Roberto and Amadeo

Amadeo and Rosetta in their kitchen before it was modernized

bells sounded out the well-known dirge. I was in the olive grove, just below the church, and stopped to watch the huge bell swinging up in the campanile. It was incredibly moving to witness this time-honored way of signaling the passing of a life, the passage of a human being into the realm of spirit. Although Amadeo was 90 years old and had come to the end of his natural life, there was something about the way life and death are played out in this little corner of Italy that seems so in sync with the rhythms of nature and the passing of the seasons. And how wonderful to be honored with a tolling bell, to be seen as a member of the community whose time has come, to have your passing marked by a public notice such as this, rather than an e-mail or a few lines in the newspaper.

Everyone knew for whom this bell tolled. Amadeo had been in the hospital for a few days and it was obvious he wouldn't be coming home. I reflected that he may be one of the last generations in Italy to have his birth celebrated by a chiming bell, his marriage by joyous peals, and his death by the tolling of the same bells. He had lived in this tiny mountain village his whole life, apart from a spell in Belgium after the war when he was a miner, as there was no work to be found in Italy. He was born here, and returned here after the war and became a *contadino*, tending his grapes and olives and *orto*, providing for himself and his family, and contributing heart and soul to the wellbeing of the community. He was also just about the last of the *vecchi*, the old men of the village. Apart from our neighbor Sergio, the village is now made up mostly of widows. His widow Rosetta cannot drive, so that is a problem—he used to drive her everywhere. Their two sons are oil company geologists, both living in the city at least three hours away, so we wonder how Rosetta will manage.

Rosetta and Lina at the grocery van which visits the village every week

Porcini Hunting In Tuscany

October 2013

THIS TIME OF YEAR in Tuscany it's all about mushrooms—hunting them, cooking them and eating them—though they can be eaten raw. I hadn't been a big *porcini* fan up until now, but their distinct wild, woodsy flavor grows on you—and after all, there is a sense of exclusiveness and rarity about them: they only grow wild, under certain conditions, in certain parts of the country side, at a certain time of year. Yes, you can buy them dried, but there is nothing like fresh *porcini*.

This season started like all others—the locals shaking their heads, pursing their lips and looking up at the sky, saying it's too warm/wet/cold for a good mushroom season. *Que peccato!* What a shame! But then the weather turns to rain, and on the first dry morning, we see our neighbors sneaking into the woods with little baskets to hunt for the elusive fungi.

Porcini are mushrooms of the boletus species, so called because they resemble a small pig, or piglets—*porco* = pig, *porcino* = small pig, with *porcini* being the plural form. They grow shrouded with leaves under ancient oak and chestnut trees, and there are plenty of those around here—we are in northern Tuscany, surrounded by forests and rushing streams, rather than in the south with the more classic and familiar Tuscan landscape of undulating fields, bleached-white unpaved roads, and groves of cypress trees.

On Sunday we went with some Italian friends to the local restaurant for their annual *porcini* festa, where, like little piglets, we pigged out on the elusive fungi. There was pasta with *porcini*, or a raw mushroom salad, to start, fillet steak or veal with *porcini* for the main course, and a side dish of deep-fried *porcini*, tempura style. I told our friends that one of Cape Cod's most famous dishes is fried clams, *vongole fritte*, and they thought that was a great idea. Why hadn't anyone thought of that before? Thankfully, no one had thought of porcini ice cream, and dessert was delicious *panna cotta* (literally cooked cream).

Rosetta with a huge porcini mushroom that she found deep in the woods; she is the champion mushroom hunter of the village and keeps her hunting grounds a closely-guarded secret!

Porcini are quick and simple to cook: slice thin, saute in olive oil, season to taste, and toss in a handful of chopped garlic and parsley, and *ecco presto!* it's done—delicious served over pasta. Cooking might take only a few minutes, but hunting them can take hours and you realize why they sell at the market stalls for up to $30 a pound. On the weekends, our country lanes are filled with cars of city people coming to the countryside to hunt for mushrooms, but unless they know where to look, they will go home with no more than a basket-full of chestnuts. The locals like to go it alone—they know where to look, and jealously guard their favorite spots.

Our final guests of the season at the villa, a delightful family from Australia, had been out early one morning and had come across our neighbor Pino who was furtively mushroom hunting in the

Easter lunch with former neighbors Pino and Mima at their new apartment in Fivizzano

depths of the woods. Pino had given them a mushroom—which is like giving someone a piece of gold—and they had just got back to the house when he arrived with a small bag full, which was extremely generous of him. We take our neighbors Pino and his wife Mima to the market every Tuesday, as they don't have a car, and they repay us however they can, usually with fresh eggs, but this time, with *porcini*. We cooked them up that evening, with plenty of garlic, parsley and olive oil, and we all gathered at the long table under the grape arbor for the last outdoor meal of the season, lingering long into the night over *biscotti* and *vin santo*. The children had initially said they didn't want any pasta with mushrooms, but when they'd tasted it, they came asking for more! Sadly, there were no more that evening, we'd eaten every last morsel, but I was glad that it was not only I who was a convert to the mystique of these very special mushrooms.

. . .

GUEST COMMENT:

"We have had such an amazing, relaxing time in this
beautiful villa set in the most breathtaking surroundings.
I cannot begin to describe how sad I am at leaving,
and how I could easily stay to look out at the mountains
and sit by the pool listening to the silence.
It is utterly beautiful."

— *Annabel from England*

The "Free" House

IT ALL BEGAN AT LUNCH one day at Spino Fiorito when Riccardo, after having ordered a second bottle of wine with lunch and then knocking back a liqueur for good measure, courtesy of the hostelry, declared that Dario was giving away a house. At first we didn't understand what he was saying in his broken English. Sometimes it's better if he sticks to Italian. The house is a present, he kept saying. *"E grande, anche, 3,000 metri quadrati."* I still have a hard time converting square meters into square feet, so I have no concept of how large this is. It's in the old part, *l'antico borgo*, of Castilioncello, the hillside village directly across the valley from our tiny village of Reusa. *"'Ee geeves eet as a geeft,"* he says. *"Un regalo."* Finally it dawns on us: Dario is giving away the house for free. Apparently, it was under agreement to a company in Bergamo who was going to convert it into three apartments, but then the earthquake hit in June and the house was severely damaged. No one wants to buy a damaged building, especially in our area, where the earthquake level has now been raised from orange to red—and may stay that way for five to ten years, according to Riccardo. It's good time buy property, he says. So we agree to take a look at the house We have visions of fixing up a little town-house—getting it for nothing, taking our time with the renovations, and selling it after five or ten years, or whenever the climate is more favorable for selling a place in Northern Tuscany.

I have already voiced my stipulations—I am not interested in property that is north facing and has no land; apart from that, I have an open mind. After lunch the next day, we drive up to Castillioncello, where I've never been before—although for ten years I've been looking directly at it across the valley from our house—and squeeze our

car into the sharp curve on the winding country road that leads to
Pieve di Offiano, the local parish church, and then on to Castillioncello. We hail Dario and walk together up the mule path that wends
through the old *borgo,* arriving at an imposing stone building at
the far end. My heart sinks. North facing, no land. But it's a beautiful house inside, more like a small palace, but between earthquake
damage and negligence—it's been pretty much empty for 40 or 50
years, no one is quite sure—the once exquisite building is in ruins.
A leaking roof has caused rotten beams, sagging floors, bulging
walls, and water-logged tiles and plaster—*un disastro*, in fact. And
it's huge, rambling across a kind of bridge over the village lane into
another house, with so many rooms we can't count them. But we
note the vaulted ceilings, carved stone porticos, faded painted ceilings, ancient stone staircases, and the carved stone vats in the *cantina*
for holding olive oil. It must be 400 or 500 years old. All in all, it is
a tragic site, because no one is going to come up with the million or
so euros that it would take to repair the damage. And it makes me

Roberto's barn before renovation

Another view of Roberto's barn before renovation

angry. We felt the same way about the house we just finished reno-vating—we are stunned at the lack of concern for these beautiful old houses, part of Italy's rich heritage. This must have once been the home of the local *signore* and his family for centuries—how could SOMEONE not have had the impulse, the desire, to at least fix the roof so the place wasn't ruined? It's unfathomable to me. Sometimes I think it's only the English and the Americans who care enough to fork out the dough to restore old Italy to its former glory, and no one else gives a damn.

A nice little terraced house and barn at the other end of the *borgo* has just been bought by some Scandinavians, Dario tells us. Of course, it's a ruin, and they are about to embark on the very expensive process of taking it down to its bare bones—its stone walls—and putting in new floors, new windows and doors, all the utilities. And of course, most expensive of all, a new roof which costs so much because of the anti-seismic fortifications. Which is what we did with our old ruin, now a beautiful villa; we used to joke and call our house Casa di Cimento (the Cement House), because there are literally tons of cement fortifying the foundations—in fact, the house is bolted to the bedrock of the mountain it stands on. But now we are glad, because we had scarcely a fracture in the plaster walls after the earthquake, while other houses around us were severely damaged—most often houses renovated by their Italian owners on the cheap, without proper plans, trying to evade the stringent rules, but their new roofs and repairs didn't withstand the earthquake. Our neighbor who repaired his roof a few years ago by this old-time method is now facing a bill of around 50,000 euros for having to install steel beams and nuts and bolts to hold his house together.

We shake our heads and remark that only a fool would take on a project like this. But it gets us thinking. Maybe someone else has a house they want to get rid of, but a bit smaller? In another *borgo*,

Roberto's barn and aia after renovation

maybe, one that is south-facing and has some land? Apparently, property isn't selling in this area because of the earthquake warning. Yes, it would be a good time to buy.

And then the quarterly bank statement arrives, always an opportunity for us to review the expenses of running this place in Italy. After entering the figures in a spreadsheet, we realized how much we are paying for electricity. Yikes! It must be three or four thousand euros a year! We expect it to be high in the summer, when the pump for the swimming pool is on and the house is full of visitors, but it's high even in the winter. What can we do? It's been a very sunny winter—in fact, there's been no winter at all to speak of. So what about solar power? What about putting photo voltaic panels on the roof of the barn? And can't we then sell the electricity back to the grid? That's what Rosetta's son Marcello has done—even when he's not here, his house is making money for him by generating electricity. We look at the barn and realize that in order to do that, we need to replace the roof. And then it dawns on us that if we replace the roof, we might as well do the floors and the walls . . . and make it into a little house. We don't need to look for more property! We have our own barn to convert right here.

Letter to our friend Jim

October 2014

Ciao Jim, caro amico:

Ginny and Gary arrived here last Thursday and spent a few days with us after delivering the items I had forgotten and which you so kindly retrieved from our house and gave to them to bring here. It was great to see them, but honestly, I have not been feeling well since I got here and came down with that virus; my voice is still weak and an evening of eating and talking and drinking just wears me out, it feels more like an ordeal than a pleasure. Riccardo asked us out for dinner on Saturday evening with his family and some friends at a new *agriturismo* way out in the country—there were twelve of us, and it was the usual Italian evening, starting at eight, bright lights overhead all the better to see the food, with kids running around, one only three years old, people on cell-phones, everyone walking around talking to one another, arguing, going outside for a smoke, and spending at least 10 minutes discussing each course before ordering . . . three hours later we left, exhausted. Fun but not something I can do every weekend! One of the women, Monica, who cleans our villa in the summer season, has asked us for dinner at her house this Saturday for *gamberone* (large shrimp) but I am wondering whether to decline. Ginny and Gary will be in Venice next week and have asked us if we'd like to join them, and I am still debating it.

One of the reasons is that I finally got to the dentist yesterday evening. The appointment was at 6 pm for three of us—Riccardo and Ron and me. They actually didn't have time to see Ron but squeezed me in, the dentist himself giving my teeth a cleaning with the Wa-

109

terpik in one hand and talking on the *telefonino* with the other, very
cavalier, like the George Clooney of Massa-Carrara, young and tall
and slim, rushing from one exam room to another—but very com-
petent all the same, *speriamo* (let's hope so). I took him the x-rays
Ralph [we both go to the same dentist in the US] had taken (which
had cost me twice as much as they do here) and he got them right up
on the computer screen, gave them some considerable thought, as
I'd told him that my US dentist thought there was some decay there,
that the fillings were too big to be removed and replaced, and therefore I'd have to have three crowns, and that would be $5,400. Which
is why I went to an Italian dentist to get a second opinion. So I was
glad to hear he thought they were okay, and he thinks the wait-and-
watch approach will be fine. But he said that I had some periodontal
disease around my bridge, which is at least 15 years old, so I have
to go back for a treatment next Monday which means we might not
be able to make the trip to Venice. It's only about a four-hour drive
which seems so close! Can you imagine? The most beautiful city in
the world is only a four-hour drive away . . .

I went to the local commune today to apply for residency, and took
all the appropriate paperwork, but it seems now that you need health
insurance from another country—my national health card from the
UK is not acceptable here. So that's a bummer. I guess too many im-
migrants have arrived here with health problems. After that, I went
to the local shop to buy some honey, and Antonella told me that
there's very little honey around, the bees are dying. Not here too! I
thought. Argh. And the chestnut trees are infected too, they are dying. So it's a disaster all around. But Maurizio says that they found an
insect that is an antidote to the insect that is causing the infection in
the chestnut trees that's working in the south, so maybe our landscape can be saved.

Anyway, that's the news from here . . . apart from the fact that I woke
to the sound of cowbells this morning, and three of the herd from

across the valley had found their way across the stream and up the hill to our meadow and were contentedly grazing on the other side of Sebastiano's *orto*, his vegetable plot. The other day the herd (or flock?) of goats, all 19 with bells on, were in our olive grove, and I wondered how it would sound if they all came up together, it would be quite a country symphony of bells.

It's still warm here—I just got bitten by a mosquito on the hand, damn, and I'm in the house! I hope all is well with you and you are having nice fall weather. Let me know your news—thinking of you!

Love, Gillian

Jim and Gillian chipping cement off Roberto's barn during his visit in 2005

Lost in Lunigiana

January 2014

AS WE SPED TOWARDS our little mountain village and had just turned off the main road for the last couple of miles of the journey, we were startled to see a massive 16-wheeler backing down the narrow country road towards us. As we screeched to a halt, a young man jumped out, plainly glad to see someone who might know the area. It was obvious he was lost. He spoke no English, no French, and only one word of Italian: *autostrada*. Then he pointed to himself and said, Polak. He was a long way from home, several countries away, in fact. We backed our car into a nearby driveway and helped him maneuver his huge rig down to the main road. Thank heavens he hadn't gone any farther, or he would never have been able to back up, nor turn around; the road around the next bend had a deep ravine along one side and a sheer rock cliff on the other. So we pointed him in the direction of the autostrada, 30 minutes down the mountain road, and could only wonder what he was doing so far from home without a map or GPS, and not a word of any language but his own. Maybe those old Polish jokes have more truth in them than we thought . . .

Ron walking back to the villa on the country road after lunch at Spino Fiorito

A Visit from Roberto and Velia

October 25th, 2014

WHEN ROBERTO AND VELIA arrive, it's as if a whirlwind has blown through the house. They are a delightful couple who were our former neighbors; now they live in Carrarra, near the Mediterranean. They used to rent a tiny stone cottage from our neighbor Sergio, until he, in his dotage, decided they should pay the taxes as well as the rent, and they had a falling out. Meanwhile, they had stored their stuff in our barn until they found another suitable rental, but so far they hadn't been able to find anything. We miss them—they are lively and personable, and speak an Italian we can understand, unlike our neighbors who mostly converse in dialect and only learned Italian at school as a second language.

We'd had guests arrive the day before—our friends Ginny and Gary had stopped off for the night on their way back from Venice—and just as they were leaving on Saturday morning to drive back to Spain, where they were staying for the winter, we had a phone call from Velia telling us they were leaving in half an hour with *rostaticcia* for lunch and would be there by noon. Ron and I looked at each other, eyebrows arching in a question that said, Did YOU invite them for the weekend? Neither of us could remember, but when Velia talks on the phone, sometimes we don't quite understand all of what she is saying. So we shrugged our shoulders and told her we were looking forward to seeing them. It's always an adventure when they arrive for a visit. We quickly changed the sheets on their bed, tidied up the house, and waited for lunch time.

They arrived with armfuls of food—sausages, pork spare ribs, and chicken from their local butcher in Carrarra, fresh bread, a large pot of Velia's own bottled wild mushrooms, beet greens, and salad—all the fixings for a barbecue, Italian style. We supplied the wine. And the fire.

Roberto likes to cook the old-fashioned way. He used to live next door and we are care-taking for him a rickety barbecue grill that he made from bits of scrap metal and old cooker grills. As soon as he arrived, he dragged it out of our chestnut drying-house onto the stone courtyard and started a fire with bits of paper, quickly achieving a blaze with twigs from our winter wood pile. On went a baking pan full of raw meat and he was a happy man, swigging wine out of a glass in one hand, and wielding a large fork in the other, smiling from ear to ear. This is an outdoorsman who now lives in an small apartment and he's blissfully happy to be back in the beauty and freedom of the countryside.

It's a glorious summer's day in late October; what a joy to be able to eat outside! Velia and I set the table under the grape arbor and

Roberto and his make-shift barbecue

Roberto and Ron carousing

prepare the vegetables and salad and soon Roberto announces that lunch is ready. Another languid lunch, Italian style, though I am beginning to feel like a stuffed pig.

For dessert, we decide to go to the chestnut festival at a neighboring village, Regnano, set higher up in the hills from Reusa, one of the last villages before the landscape changes to the mountainous terrain of the Emilia-Romano Alps. By this time next year, our area should officially be part of this national park, says our neighbor Maurizio. And that would be good for the area, he tells us, because it's a national park, and that means we'll get money to help preserve it.

The *festa* was held in a field just below the village, set with buildings especially for events such as these—and Regnano, with its rich history, has many of them. A long building with an impressive kitchen, all stainless steel as per the new EU regulations, forms one side of a square field. Next to it is a little stage that had been transformed into a tableaux of what a kitchen would have looked like in the old days, probably not more then 50 years ago, and another building, three-sided, rather like a bus stop, which probably serves as a stadium for watching impromptu football matches. This is where local people had set up their hand-made wares to sell. Under a grove of chestnut trees were demonstrations by villagers showing how, in the not-too-distant past, they relied on chestnuts as a major part of their sustenance. There was chestnut roasting, chestnut peeling, and a demonstration of the grinding of chestnuts into flour, all carried out by locals dressed for the occasion in old-fashioned clothes, and a variety of foods made from chestnuts—polenta, breads, cakes, pancakes—being cooked up in the kitchen.

We stood in line and paid for our choices—we ordered *cian*, a chestnut pancake normally filled with *ricotta* cheese, but they'd run out of *ricotta*, which Roberto found derisible, even though the substitute cream cheese was more delicious than *ricotta*. He is hard to please; Italians are such traditionalists. I had ordered a *frittelon*, impossible to describe really, but a kind of baked pancake of chestnut flour containing raisins. We were tasting the delicacies and sampling the local wine when Roberto noticed that the *frittelon* did not have rosemary and pine nuts in it, as the photo at the ordering booth had shown, so he complained to the worthy ladies who were slaving away in the kitchen cooking all these different foods. One of them came to our table to explain that their recipe was different, and anyway, who could afford pine nuts these days? As they continued their passionate argument about food and how it should be cooked, I gazed out of the window and watched some local children running about in a playground, a couple of swings set on a grassy slope shaded by chestnut trees, with an incredible view of the Apuan Alps in the distance. I thought how lucky they were to be raised in such a beautiful place, and hoped they appreciated it.

The next morning, Ron and Roberto decided to burn some brush down in the valley. A spiral of smoke drifted up the hillside as I walked Pepe down to join them. As I wended my way through the olive grove, I heard the sound of loud voices, heated voices. This is Italy and people do tend to get passionate, but this sounded different, and

I realized this was an altercation. Apparently, Miralda had just hung out her washing and was expressing her displeasure. Unfortunately, she expressed it to Roberto, who has a short temper, and a slanging match started. We don't know exactly what was said, but we do know that Miralda's husband Sebastiano, the man who loves growing things, had recently bought a coveted piece of land that Roberto, now a city dweller, had had his eye on. It would have been perfect for him, he had told us, with terraces for a small vineyard, a few olive trees, and a little barn where they could stay overnight—even though that was illegal. But the owner of the land decided she wanted to sell her land to someone who lived in the village, and she chose Sebastiano. I don't know if some of this rancor came out in their angry shouting match, but Ron decided the best approach was to extinguish the fire and wait for a day when Miraldo didn't have her washing hanging out on the line.

But the incident left a kind of pall on the day. We are all neighbors, living close by each other for over ten years, helping each other out when necessary, and this was a very unusual occurrence. But later that day, when Ron was working down in the laundry room, Miralda, who is the church warden, came by after locking up the church and apologized profusely, and surprised him by giving him a hug. Obviously the incident had been weighing on her too. We are glad they made up, but now we know that when we see a line of washing hanging outside her house, it's like a red flag that says: no burning!

When Roberto and Velia left, we were exhausted from trying to speak Italian non-stop for two days. Much as we love them, and much as we are interested in improving our speaking skills, we find that we get to the point that there's just not enough room in our heads for any more. So it was with relief that we were able to sit in front of the TV and watch an old episode of Agatha Christie's Poirot—in English. We may have seen it several times before, but it was like salve for our over-taxed brains. And it made us wonder if we'll ever become fluent in Italian.

The Silence of the Bells

April 26th, 2014

I WAS AWAKENED AT 7 am in the morning on Friday, April 18th, which was Good Friday. This was a surprise as the bells should have been silenced. Why were the bells ringing on this holy day when there should only be silence for a solemn church vigil to commemorate Christ's crucifixion? I found out when I saw Miralda walking by the house. The vigil was being kept in the church in Codiponte, she told me. This was the first time that there had been no traditional Easter vigil kept at the little church in Reusa. Was this because of the earthquake damage from the summer before? Or because there were now so few people left in the village that there really was no point? But if that was the case, how could the few remaining villagers, mostly widows who did not drive, get to Codiponte, a good five miles away? Maybe church activities were becoming a smaller and less important part of village life as time marched on.

But there was good news—the Easter service was being held on Sunday, at 11:15 am. Usually, the weekly mass was held on Saturday afternoon, a very inconvenient time when most people are sleeping off their lunch. The very odd tune that is played on the church's three bells to announce the coming service is enough to wake anyone out of a sound sleep. I have a recording of our dog Pepe howling at the cacophony. The reason for this is that Daniele, the local priest, has five village churches to get around to, and he just can't do it all on one day, no matter how fast he drives and how speedily he gets through the prayers. So this Easter our village has decided to hire a vigilante—a private priest—so they can have the service on a Sunday. Unfortunately, we will miss it, as we've been invited by our friends and former neighbors Pino and Mima for Easter lunch at their home in Fivizzano. But we are glad that our neighbors will be able to celebrate Mass on Easter, to celebrate Christ's rising from the dead on the appropriate day, and not the day before.

The next day, walking back from the local restaurant after lunch, I heard a familiar sound that had been missing since I'd returned a few weeks before—cowbells! The cows were back in their pasture after spending the winter months in a barn, and now their bells rang out over the valley, as they had done ever since we'd arrived in this village more than ten years before. They were frisky, chasing each other about the field in their first taste of freedom in months, and the clanging and chiming sounded timeless.

The day after *Pasquetta*—"little Easter" or Easter Monday—when everything was back to normal after the hectic Easter weekend, we were that Daniele would be coming around the village to bless the houses. We'd always had our house blessed, giving a generous donation to the church for the process, but this year, we made double sure we were home when he called—after last year's horrendous earthquake, we needed all the protection we could get.

At the allotted hour, he came to the house, all smiles and friendliness. We are so lucky to have him as a priest, after the assortment of odd-balls we've had in the past—a visiting priest from Ghana, a retired plumber who'd taken his vows late in life, and an adorable and very gay young man from some eastern European country with a blond Beatles haircut—Daniele was the real thing: charming, earnest, intelligent, and empathetic—and Italian. And he loved to practice his English. After he'd sprinkled holy water about the house and gratefully taken our donation, he mentioned something about the old *canonica*—the former priests' house that is positioned next to the church and is surrounded on three sides by our olive grove. We nearly fell down right in front of him. We had wanted to buy the

The ruined canonica

old *canonica* ten years ago but the village council, made up mostly of the old ladies of the village, had told us that they'd rather leave it as a ruin than sell it to someone who'd fix it up and might rent it out to foreigners—even Germans; memories of the war still linger here and negative feelings towards the Germans run deep. So we forgot about buying it, and have watched it decay and rot before our eyes as the beams gave way and the roof fell in, the stone walls now held up only by ivy as thick as a man's wrist.

But, according to Daniele, things had changed. The new *canonica*, which the parish council had built with the money they'd got when the old *canonica* had been damaged in the earthquake of 1920, had itself been damaged in the earthquake of 2013. And it would cost a lot to repair. He mentioned a figure of 50,000 euros and suggested that we might like to consider purchasing the old *canonica* to enable the parish council to repair the new priest's house. The reason for this is that they rent out the priest's house, since the priest does not need

to live in it any more—he lives in the nearby village of Codiponte—
and the rental income pays for the expenses for the church and for
the electricity for the lights that illuminate the church and campanile
so they can be seen at night from miles away. So they need to fix the
new *canonica* to get the income to maintain the church. Whether
Daniele actually said they wanted 50,000 euros for it, or whether that
amount was mentioned merely to impress upon us the severity of the
damage and the urgent need of funds, we were not sure. But it was a
starting point for negotiations. And we were interested—boy, were
we interested. The building is of historical significance, with a date of
1642 carved in stone over the front door, and our olive grove abut-
ted it on three sides, making it undesirable property to anyone but
ourselves. It would be crazy not to buy it. Or maybe it would be crazy
to buy it? It would have to be virtually demolished and rebuilt. That
would take time . . . and money.

**Daniele the priest officiating at the wedding of Gabriella and Davide
(of Spino Fiorito) at the church in Reusa**

The first thing we did was talk to Riccardo, who has a very practical head upon his broad shoulders. He didn't dismiss the idea as crazy, so that was encouraging. But he did say that Vittorio, our *geometra*, was coming to inspect the house he was working on in the village that very afternoon, and he'd bring him by to take a look at the old ruin after work. Things were moving very fast all of a sudden. Did we really want to take on another renovation project? It seemed that things might be out of our hands, yet again . . .

Vittorio took one look at the ruin and said, basically, I hope they are giving this to you as a gift. When we explained the situation, he suggested a price of 15,000 euros as being fair, 20,000 being tops, if we wanted to be generous to the church. That sounded more like it. Now we needed to get Karsten, who is German but who speaks flawless Italian and English, to do our negotiating. We'd fortuitously had him to dinner just a few days earlier to meet the German family who'd been staying in our guest quarters for a couple of weeks, so we figured he owed us one. So who knows—we might have another project in Italy to start work on, just when we thought it was all finished and we were done.

Martin and family from Germany at a barbecue at Casa della Quercia

Wine Beyond Price

Events c. April 15th • Written April 22nd, 2014

THE DAY STARTED AUSPICIOUSLY when I found a four-leaved clover, a pleasant surprise after a day that hadn't ended auspiciously at all. That day, we'd had three plumbers scratching their heads over a drainage problem with no hope, it seemed, of a resolution. And here we were the next morning, our plumber still scratching his head and trying all sorts of things to get the water to flow. So when I took a break and came face-to-face with a four-leaved clover while doing a yoga stretch on a tiny patch of lawn on the garden terrace, I felt a glimmer of hope for a better day.

We'd dug up this entire terrace last October looking for a broken pipe—which we didn't find, not in this location anyway. So the dug-up earth and rocks were all piled back into the gaping hole, creating another problem—a terrace that had to be leveled and replanted, while the plumbing problem persisted. I had spent the past week raking and leveling the ground and laying a stone path, hefting 30 flagstones into position, and I was dreading the news that we'd have to dig up the terrace again in search of the broken pipe. All that work for nothing!

And so it was, as I was stretching between pick-axe swings on this glorious April day, with the cuckoo singing its manic song from the woodland across the valley and the swallows wheeling overhead, that I received a sign from Mother Nature that things might go better today—a mutant clover leaf. And I was right. After two more hours of labor, we heard the sound of rushing water and an exultant *"E risolto!"*—it's resolved!—from the plumber and we knew we were free of that problem, at least for a while.

To celebrate, we drove into Fivizzano for a quick look around the market and to join our builders Riccardo and Andrea for lunch at a simple country ristorante nearby, Il Castello in Verrucola. We had eaten there for the first time the previous year and had enjoyed their homemade wine so much that we'd reserved a demi-john of the new vintage to keep in our *cantina*—for our guests, and for ourselves. Riccardo, who goes there for lunch when his building work happens to be nearby, had heard from Mauro, the owner and wine-maker, that the wine was ready to be picked up, so we emptied the trunk of our old Fiat Uno and set off to pick up the wine.

As we drove north over the mountain towards Fivizzano, a great black cloud appeared over the Emilia-Romano alps to the east, and we knew we were in for a squall. Sure enough, just as we walked into the market square, the heavens opened and the wind blasted through the narrow lanes, turning our umbrella inside out and sending the stall holders and their wares scurrying into their vehicles for shelter, bringing the outdoor market to an abrupt end. We were glad to reach the warmth and safety of our car without getting soaked, and headed up to Verrucola, eagerly anticipating our meal in this different location for our daily ritual of *pranzo di lavoro*—as well as sampling the new vintage of wine, which we did, though perhaps rather too enthusiastically.

Mauro had told Riccardo that we could pick up the wine after lunch at his *cantina* at his home. We assumed his *cantina* was in the same village, or maybe just around the corner . . . but no such luck. He rattled off some directions that mentioned Agnino, a little town a good six miles away, located high up above the Aulella river valley and reached by a tricky mountain road. With any luck he had meant in the direction of Agnino, or even on the road to Agnino? Wherever it was, we wanted the wine, and so after a hearty lunch washed down with plenty of the new vintage, we jumped into our beaten up old Fiat and followed Mauro along the road that lead back to Fivizzano, down through the beautiful valley to the west, and then up into the hills. And he had meant Agnino. He led us up a winding mountain road, only one car wide in some places, and with a precipitous drop on the valley side—not for the faint hearted, nor the slightly inebriated. Wishing that we'd drunk a little less of the wine we were now in search of, we screwed up our courage and followed his truck up the hill, past mountain meadows of buttercups and olive groves full of wild flowers. Ron spotted a car that had gone off the road and had ended up in the ravine below, and he gripped the wheel even more tightly. Finally we reached Agnino, high up on a mountain crest overlooking the plain below, with a spectacular view of cascading mountain ranges reaching as far as the sea to the west.

Finally, we reached his *podere*, his small farm, with vineyards and olive groves and a modest house presiding over it all, and took possession of the precious wine. We headed home in a happy mood—the sun had returned and the rainstorm had washed the countryside so it looked more beautiful than ever, buttercups shining like gold, and with the occasional scarlet spot of an early field poppy. Half an hour later we arrived home, glad to be back in one piece. Our neighbor Maurizio happened to be passing so he helped us carry the demijohn into the *cantina*, but we decided were too distracted to decant it and Ron thought that a little nap might be necessary. But no sooner had he laid his head down than two visitors arrived at the door.

The visitors were Cameron and his friend Pete. Ron had met Cameron, a fellow American, before, but not Pete, who was British, and I had met neither. But I had been up to see Cameron's house many times, a charming old farmhouse looking out over the mountain village of Regnano, on the off-chance that Cameron might be at home. But I'd never caught a glimpse of him. Now he was here for two weeks, he told us, so we could get acquainted and swap notes on renovating old Italian ruins. I asked them in and offered them a cup of tea, but it turned out they'd prefer wine. They'd come to visit us after a leisurely lunch at Spino Fiorito, and were obviously still thinking in terms of a post-prandial glass of *vino* rather than accepting the fact that it was closer to tea time. We did have some very good wine, we told them, but it needed to be decanted. We led them into the *cantina* where they helped Ron heft the full demijohn onto the counter and emptied its contents into the stainless steel vat. We all had a taste—yes! it was just as wonderful as we'd hoped it would be!—and stayed for a while in the cool cantina, catching up and swapping stories, Ron recounting some of his adventures as a safari tour guide in Africa, and Cameron telling us about his Italian building project. He'd bought the place in 2006 and had been making small improvements as time went by, but now, after a two-year hiatus involving a nasty divorce, he'd decided to move ahead with serious renovations, especially after the damage from last year's earthquake. He asked about our builders and we told them we'd bring them up to Regnano the next day, after work. Our neighbor Lina then came calling for us, as Pete had parked his large English station wagon right in the middle of the lane, opposite Miralda's house, and she had complained that she couldn't walk her wheelbarrow past it. She didn't want to complain about it to us directly, as she didn't speak any English, and didn't want to upset us. We understood completely, it was *pazzo*, crazy, to park your car in the middle of the village lane, but it was *dopo pranzo*, after lunch, when many indiscretions can be forgiven. Pete moved his car and peace was restored. And then they had another glass of wine while we showed them around the grounds. When they left, they were definitely a bit the worst for wear, especially Pete, who was driving his English car with the steering wheel on the "wrong" side of the car. We silently prayed that they'd make it up the mountain roads and safely home.

The next day after work we drove Riccardo and Andrea up to Regnano and on to the tiny village of Poggio, a series of old stone houses jumbled around the ravine of a cascading torrent. The rivers here are called *torrente* because they run hard in winter, spring and fall, and all but dry up in summer, being fed by rainfall and snow from the mountains. We parked the car at the foot of the steep village and followed the old mule path up through the ancient *borgo* and to the mountain meadows and vineyards that lie above it.

Cameron's house is the last house on the mountain path, sitting square in the middle of a beautiful meadow, so flat that you'd never know we were at nearly 2000 feet. The house is undeniably charming, with heavy old beams and a kitchen that remained just as it had when the last owners left—a massive stone fireplace charred black, old marble sink, and rustic wooden cupboards. The house was furnished with heavy Italianate furniture that might look clunky in another setting, but here added to the sense of perfection. This was a house that you need to do as little as possible to, I remarked . . . and our builder Riccardo was the one to do that, being not just a builder but also an artist. We sat around the kitchen table and talked back and forth in a mixture of Italian and English over a couple of glasses

The kitchen at Cameron's house

of local wine, discussing what needed to be done to the house. As I said to Cameron, all it needs it to be made safe (thinking of last summer's earthquake), and watertight, since there were hints of mold in the air after a particularly rainy winter.

Riccardo had to get back home to drive his young son to a football match, so we said our goodbyes and set off on the mountain path back to the village. Suddenly, we were hailed from a field behind a hedge—it was Valerio, who worked at the *comune* in Casola with Maurizio and whose father had just left him a house in this village when he died, and Pierino, who takes care of our olive grove. They had been working in Valerio's vineyard and *orto*, getting the soil ready to plant tomatoes, and were now sitting on a makeshift wooden bench sampling the first of the new season's wine while the detritus from the vineyard was smoldering in a fire behind them. At

I ragazzi at Cameron's house

times there was so much smoke swirling around that we could barely
see them. They invited us to join them, and we soon found ourselves
sitting in a circle around the fire sampling the wine. It was excellent, probably the best wine we've ever tasted. Valerio explained it
was made from San Giovese grapes, the most common grape in this
area, and some Merlot. But there was another flavor I recognized,
one of my favorites—that of blackberry and cherry. And *cileogiollo*,
I suggested? *Esatto!* exclaimed Valerio. The wine was divine, we all
agreed. If I continue on like this, Riccardo commented, my wife will
be wondering what I'm getting up to after work! I asked Valerio if he
would consider selling us demijohn of this wine but he laughed and
shook his head; he had two brothers who loved to drink his wine.
His brothers are high-ranking officers in the military who had gone
on to distinguished careers while he'd stayed home to take care of his
father and work in a clerical job at the local town hall. His father had
died the summer before, at the age of 90, soon after he and Valerio
had renovated his huge old stone house with its nine bedrooms.
Valerio had inherited the house just before the earthquake hit this
remote village, severely damaging the majority of the houses. The
front part of the house that he'd renovated was undamaged, but the
outhouses and *cantine* in the back had been rendered unsafe, and the
cost for repair was close to 40,000 euros. If his father had lived just
a month longer, they would have had some money from the state to
help with the repairs. But because at the time of the earthquake, the
house had belonged to Valerio and was technically his second house,
there would be no help from the government. So for now the house
sits uninhabited, like so many in this region. Only the wealthy can
afford to renovate. But Valerio still keeps up the house as best he can,
and takes care of the land, making this delicious wine using the same
traditional method as his father had done, and his father before him.
This is the kind of wine that money can't buy, I thought, as was the
experience of sitting around a campfire on the warm earth as the sun
slipped behind the mountains. These are the best experiences of all, I
realized—even if we couldn't buy any wine to take away with us, we

Pierino pouring the wine in Valerio's vineyard

could take away that indelible memory, that moment in time when friends met in a country field and shared some sustenance, a ritual as old as time.

By some strange coincidence, the next day our neighbor Sergio collared Ron and asked him if he wanted any wine. Ron had mentioned last autumn that he'd like to buy a demijohn of his homemade wine, and now it was ready. Ron had forgotten this, but there was Sergio, 80 years old and six feet tall, with his loud gravelly voice, pushing a wheelbarrow made of ancient zinc tied together with white string, and in it, a demijohn of his red wine. Delighted and surprised, we directed him into our *cantina*, which turned out to be a much shorter and more convenient method of wine delivery than having to drive to Agnino. Ron and Sergio wrestled the wine out of the wheelbarrow and onto the bare floor of the *cantina*, and then we asked how much we owed him. Sergio took a seat on an old chair and assumed the posture of someone about to discuss serious business. He said something to Ron that he just didn't understand. I wasn't paying attention, as I thought it would just be a simple case of, That's 80 euros, or some such sum. But we were wrong. Nothing is simple with Sergio. He is the patriarch of the village, now that Lina's husband Roberto has passed on. He owns most of the land and all the little houses around that are for rent, as well as his fine property that is perched on the terrace above our house. He repeated what he had said, and I fortunately picked up some key words and realized he wasn't asking for money, he wanted to cut down some oak trees at the edge of our olive grove in return for the wine. He assured us he wouldn't cut down any more trees than the wine was worth. That raised the question, what is an oak tree worth? They are not large oak trees, more like a kind of scrub oak that when felled and chopped up make small logs about 2" in diameter that are perfect for the wood stoves that many people in the mountains use for heating their homes, imported gas from Russia being way too expensive. The word for oak is *quercia*, the name of our village, but *cera* is what the locals call this small oak tree. Which he actually called a plant, a *piante*, not a tree, *albero*. No wonder Ron was confused. *Cera* also means wax, and *c'era* means "it was"—even more confusing. But because I had understood, Sergio paid me the highest compliment, saying I was *"molto intelligente"*— or was it because he wanted me to make a deal with him? I am not sure. We felt we didn't have much choice but to agree, but we are still wondering how many oak trees we'll have to sacrifice for this wine. And we can't taste the wine yet, because all our stainless steel vats are now full. Pierino had given us a demijohn of homemade white wine, slightly *frizzante* and tasting of muscat grapes, made by a friend of his, and that had gone into our spare metal container. So to taste Sergio's wine we will have to go the hardware store and buy another container, which would probably cost more than the wine itself. So we were being asked to sacrifice some oak trees for wine we haven't yet tasted! Yet more wine that is beyond price, I thought . . . and yet another experience that is priceless, here in Italy, living *la bella vita*.

La Dolce Vita

May 2015

I WAS WATCHING A TV program about an English couple a few days ago who were looking for an old farmhouse to fix up and live in in Abruzzo, and I wondered why they'd want to do that, so far from anywhere of interest in Italy. They said they wanted to immerse themselves in the Italian lifestyle, to go to the street market, the *festas*, be involved in Italian everyday life. What is the draw, I wondered? Is that something I had wanted? It may have been, though in 12 years of having this house, the longest period I've spent here has been two months, hardly long enough to get immersed in the culture. But I wondered exactly what that is. And then I realized today that we had found it.

It was market day in Fivizzano, as it is every Tuesday, and we drove over the mountain road in hazy sunshine with a warm breeze drifting in from the south; it felt warm and dry after the rains of April. We sat in early May sunshine outside the café in the square while stout housewives did the rounds of the market with their baskets stuffed full of vegetables and dried cod and cozy slippers. The clock struck 11 and played an elaborate tune, loud enough to stop conversation. Karsten, our German friend who abandoned his home country for this one 25 years ago, remarked that the church bells are the reason the hotel on the square closed—the bells ring every half hour all day and all through the night.

On the way back to the car we stopped in the butcher's shop, the one that has a farm farther up the mountain in Sassalbo, and bought steaks and sausages for a barbecue later that day. The owners are so delightful—friendly and always smiling, and often giving us tips on how to cook the meat, which comes in such different cuts than we are used to in the UK or in the US. Then a stop in the little supermarket to pick up some essentials, and back in the car for the short trip to our local restaurant, Spino Fiorito, for lunch with Riccardo and his workers.

This may be the biggest difference between Europe and the US—here, the lifestyle matters more than making money, whereas in the US making money trumps all. In this part of Tuscany, everything stops at midday for lunch—no eating a sandwich on the job; work stops for at least an hour, if not one and a half, or maybe two, or even three—*dopo pranzo* can often mean at 3 o'clock—so workmen can relax over a proper meal with wine, and then, refreshed, can return to work invigorated to finish the projects for the day. The words *ristorante* comes from the word *ristoro*—to be restored, and that's what the restaurants do: they are restorative. After a *pranzo di lavoro* I feel I can take on the world. Today we were offered a choice of two types of pasta or a salad to start, for the main course there was a rolled leg of lamb stuffed with artichokes, or a mixture of grilled wild boar and pork ribs, or roast chicken, with beet greens or cannellini beans and onions, followed by *crostata* or *panna cotta*, followed by coffee and *grappa*, all washed down by local wine. Including bread and bottled water, the bill was 10 euros a piece. The restaurant was full of workmen (and a few working women) who all knew each other, and the place was full of conversation flowing from one table to the next, everyone in a good mood, troubles left at the door; this was a time to relax and enjoy an hour or so with good friends and hearty food and gentle joshing before going back to work. After the coffee, there is no lingering—an abrupt shoving back of the chairs and everyone stands up in unison to signal the end of the meal and stop by the cash register to pay for the meal—there's never a bill of course, that's what keeps it so inexpensive. The crowd moves outside and hang about the terrace or take a seat at the outdoor tables to smoke a quick cigarette and catch up on more gossip, or make a few calls on their cell phones, and then jump in their respective cars and trucks and speed off back to work.

I chose to walk back to our villa, up the hill past the olive groves, where the water fountain further up the hill overflows so there's a little stream that runs down the side of the road. It reminds me of the old days in Paris, where around Les Halles on the Left Bank the sluices would be opened up each morning and the gutters cleared by rushing water of everything from animal parts to cigarettes butts. I have always been fascinated by running water, and this walk up the hill with a little trickling stream flowing down it fills me with joy. I stop where the trees thin out and the mountain range comes into full view, and sit on the warm stones of a roadside wall to drink in the warmth of the sun and the beauty of the panorama. I've seen these mountains from many different sides, but this is the best view of all. They look balanced, in perfect symmetry, though when seen from the north, from the autostrada that leads from Genoa to Aulla, they look jagged and untidy, menacing almost. From this view point I look down on the shed where the herd of goats live, the ones that sometimes cross the steam in the valley and wander up the mountain meadow to our land, where they are usually sent running back down the mountain, bells clanging, by Pepe our dog; but once, before he came to live with us, they came up the garden path and ate two of my newly-planted cypress trees, so now I only have five, not the seven I originally planted. The cows are now in the meadow that creates a deep green streak right across the valley; I love to hear the harmo-nious clanging of their bells—larger and therefore louder than the goats, more like a sonata by Bach, the goats bells making music more like a Vivaldi concerto.

The road then takes me past Lida's olive grove, unkempt now she is getting older and no longer able to wield the hand-held scythe that she prefers to use; today it is filled with wild flowers and the silvery leaves of the olive trees tossing in the breeze. Further along, opposite the little village cemetery, where so many of our friends and Italian "family" now lie, is a steep bank that is a treasure trove of wild flowers, full of pink ragged robin, delicate violet-colored harebells, wild orchids, blue-purple wild larkspur and meadow sage, punctuated by the bright white and gold of ox-eye daisies. The poppies are blooming down in the valley along the autostrada, but not here yet. This is moment when the countryside looks its most beautiful, that fleeting moment where the grass is tall and full of flowers, but before it is mown, or falls flat and gets matted down and starts to look unkempt. The locals, the *contadini*, know exactly when to cut, leaving it as late as they can, just before it starts to fall over, but not a moment too soon, because they only want to cut it twice in the season. It's a fatiguing task, and twice in a season is enough. If it's hot enough, and not too wet, that will do, but if it's a wet season, it will have to be cut more often. And that means a lot of raking and burning, since these days there are few cattle around that need the hay.

Wild irises in the olive grove

Past the cemetery is the ravine, crossed by a stone bridge, which was blasted by the partisans in the war, much to the dismay of the locals who thought it was idiotic because it made life so difficult for everyone, not just for the Germans, and it meant reprisals. We are not sure exactly what they were, but we can only guess. Stories about war atrocities are still very much alive here; memories run deep, nothing is forgotten. The other day there was a party of tourists at Spino Fiorito that included two strapping young men, probably still teenagers, who looked Dutch or German. I couldn't help wondering if the soldiers who occupied this village in the early 1940s looked like them, with blond crew cuts and tall strong builds, so unlike the shorter, wiry and swarthier Italians.

Passing over the bridge I hear the sound of rushing water from the stream far below and then the sound of Roberto's chickens clucking and murmuring in the shade of his cherry trees, scratching up the dirt looking for worms and bugs—carnivores, like most of us, and very delicious eggs they lay too. Every time we ask if we can buy eggs, they give them to us as a gift, so it means we don't like to ask too often. I do wish Roberto and his wife Ida would let us pay for them!

Then up the hill past the ruin that used to be Ida's home during the war; her father was off fighting, her young mother left alone to take care of their young daughter, being harassed by Germans to the point where, says Ida, she "died of fright " around the age of 25, something Ida has never got over, losing her mother so young. She talks about it every time I go by to visit with her. She and her husband Roberto built a new villa next to the old house, surrounded by a beautiful garden, but the old ruin is still there as testament to the tough days of the war.

I cross another little bridge, this one not going over a river but over an old stone-paved mule path that leads down the valley and across the stream to the neighboring village of Vigneta, the main way of travel before the paved road and the bridge going over the ravine were built. The area is crisscrossed with these old stone paths—some have a name, like the Via del Volto Santo, the old Roman road and pilgrims' way that leads to Lucca and on to Rome; others connect one village to another, yet others lead up the mountains to meadows and olive groves.

On the left is the Baita, a kind of community center consisting of a hut and *bocce* court where the men of the village gather on Sundays to make a feast and drink their homemade wine and play music and card games, though the *bocce* court looks like it hasn't been used in years. And in fact, as the old-timers die off, the place is looking more and more disused; the fence is falling over, covered in wild vines, and the apple trees that line the *bocce* court are aging and decaying. Still, on occasional summer evenings, the place comes alive—smoke is

View of the Apuan Alps from the swimming pool terrace

seen drifting up from the barbecue chimney, cars arrive from other villages and line up along the roadside, and everyone makes merry and the village fills up with the sound of revels.

Our dog Pepe likes to sit in the lane that leads to our house and look through the railings to survey the road that leads to the village, rather like the Romans did from their watch towers 1500 years ago or so. He likes to look down on the Baita and Roberto's house beyond and runs down to greet friends, and sometimes strangers, and to send off stray dogs. He has often gone off on long walks with hikers, returning tired late in the day looking for his dinner. Or he'll catch the scent of a deer or wild boar and disappear into the woods, yipping in delight at the chase, and running for miles and miles, returning home flecked with spittle like a racehorse. But now that he's getting older—he's nearly five—he's becoming a little more home-bound, but when he was younger, we'd see him flying through the woods and the meadows chasing deer that looked very much like him—chestnut colored, long legged, slender built—and it seemed very much as if they were

The front courtyard of Casa della Quercia with geraniums in bloom

Pepe waiting at the gates of the villa

friends. Pepe wouldn't hurt a flea, let alone a deer, so it's all about the fun of the chase.

I see him peering down from his perch, wagging his tail in welcome, and I make the last trek up the narrow bent lane into the stone *aia* in front of the house and think how beautiful it all is, the old stone walls honey-colored in the sunshine, the pots now filled with pink geraniums ready for the summer, the grapes vines studded with budding fresh green leaves, the swallows soaring and diving overhead, washing hanging from windows, the neighbors gossiping in the lane. Yes, this is it—this is the "immersion in Italian life" that people talk about, dream about. It's nothing dramatic, nothing particularly heroic; it's in the living of daily life, what we do with our minutes and hours that make up our days, that make up our seasons, that make up the years, that make up a life; the rhythm of nature, the turning of the earth, the eternal circle of time. This is it, this is LIFE.

Italian Heat Wave

July 22nd, 2015

I AM LOVING being here in the summer. I had forgotten how much I loved it. I haven't been here for a summer holiday since 1970, and it feels just the same—the torpid heat, cool dark interiors smelling of sandalwood and ripe peaches and melons, everyone taking a siesta in the afternoon but all busy out and about at 9 and 10 pm at night, visiting, walking, enjoying the cool night air, and the church bell sounding muffled as it rings out the hour through the thickness of the heat.

This heat wave has gripped Italy like a vice, squeezing every drop of moisture out of the usually verdant countryside, turning the meadows to a crispy brown, and even the olive trees seemed to be gasping for air. The highest temperatures since 2003, said Rosetta. The hottest in 100 years, said Lina. You could cut the air with a knife. Everything and everyone slowed down, the most unlikely people appeared in public in what looked like skimpy underwear, and the lizards hid from the heat of the sun. Even the Internet service was infuriatingly slow.

All around us, ripe figs and plums plummeted to the ground, hot from the sun, and good eating if they have a soft landing—if not, they smash as they hit the road, making a mushy mess much like jam, and with no rain to wash it away, it makes for sticky footprints. The hazelnuts are already falling gently to the ground and the squirrels can't keep up with them, and the walnut trees are uncharacteristically full of bright green fruit.

We were living, though it was more like camping out, really, in our neighbor Rosetta's spare cottage, as our villa was rented out to clients.

View of the pool terrace in summer

There was no air conditioning, and with our low rent of 400 euros a month, including electricity, there was no way we could install an air conditioner; and even if we could find one, there were no sash windows as we have in the US so we could not easily install one. The last time we had an air conditioner installed in the villa, it had cost 2,000 euros and required a six-inch hole to be drilled through the three-foot thick stone wall and a separate electrical line. No, an air conditioner was out of the question. Especially in view of the fact that the fridge was on its last legs, and getting a new one installed by Marcello (Rosetta's son) was like pulling teeth. We had to keep transferring frozen ice cube trays from the freezer, which oddly enough seemed to work just fine, into the fridge and then put them back into freezer again when they had melted, in effect going back to the good old days of ice boxes.

Plus, if we installed air conditioning, there'd be nothing to complain about. The weather is the main topic of conversation among the ladies of the village. It's either too cold or too hot, or too windy, or too wet; There will be no *porcini* mushrooms in the woods this year, they warn; the olives will be ruined by the flies that weren't killed in the mild winter; the spring hail storms will damage the apple blossoms and there'll be no fruit this year; the grapes will rot on the vines from all the rain; and so it goes.

And so we are suffering through this heat wave with just a fan and judicious use of the heavy window shutters which we open at night after the sun goes down and close in the morning before it rises again, keeping the cool night air firmly locked up inside the house. I imagine I might be living in the Deep South, languishing in the heat with blinds drawn in the parlor and sipping mint juleps. Instead we languish on a foam sofa, hideously covered in something that might have been fashionable in the 1960s, and sip Bellini's, pouring Prosecco over mashed ripe white peaches in champagne glasses. One could easily become addicted, but it would be an expensive habit. Another hot weather treat we recently discovered is the *shakerato*. I howled inside with laughter when I first heard the name when I asked for an iced coffee! It's a double espresso with a little sugar syrup added,

. . .

GUEST COMMENT:

"What a remarkable place, definitely the best villa
we have ever stayed at. Beautiful, incredibly well equipped,
and all in a breathtaking location.
Usually by the end of a holiday we are ready to go home, but with
this place we could happily stay on!
Can't wait for you to finish the downstairs floor
so we can come back with friends.
P.S. Our sister-in-law said you have the best view
from a toilet seat she has ever seen!"

— *Lin, Simon, George and Wendy from Wales*

shaken well with ice in a cocktail shaker until there's a nice head of foam, and poured into a cocktail glass. Delicious!

I hadn't expected to come to Italy this summer; usually I stay in the US while Ron manages the villa and takes care of our guests. But when I arrived and heard the crickets, so much louder than the Cape Cod variety, and smelled the jasmine and saw the fireflies flashing at dusk, I was immediately transported back to Fano, on the Adriatic coast, where I used to summer with my parents, and then went to on honeymoon. Those were the days—driving from London via Paris and on to Rome, running out of petrol in the days before credit cards. Oh, the adventures of one's youth!

But the adventures continue. This was an unexpected visit for me; our friend Mike from Dar es Salaam in Tanzania, who we hadn't seen in 10 years, decided to rent our villa for his 70th birthday party, with

The renovated chestnut-drying house made a sixth bedroom

his family members and friends coming from China and England, and in my case, the US. At first I was hesitant, but when I received an invitation to my uncle's 60th wedding anniversary celebration in Wales the following week, I knew I had to go, and happily could combine both events into one lovely and unexpected summer holiday.

This particular adventure started when I first arrived and saw the FOR SALE sign on a little house at the end of our lane, a house which I wish I could have bought when it was sold three years ago, but didn't have the cash at the time. I thought it would be good for Ron to have a place of his own during the summers when our villa was rented out, and a project to work on. It was bought by an Italian woman from Elba and her Scottish husband; though Ron had met them once, I had never seen them, and the place now seemed abandoned. Apparently they had separated and she was now ill, and they needed to sell the house. Fast. I immediately called the realtor and discovered that the price was far less than they had paid, and it was negotiable, as everything is in these days of a buyer's market and fear of deflation. But I always believe in leaping in where others fear to tread, so I made what I thought was a fair offer, both for her and for me, and 24 hours later she accepted it. Before I knew it, I was in the realtor's office signing papers in both Italian and English, and was on my way to owning yet another property in Italy.

Apparently our neighbor Sebastiano had put in a ridiculously low offer on the house; he didn't want strangers next door, he told Lina's son Maurizio, and planned to knock the house down for more parking. What a tragedy that would be, I thought! The house is very old, historic even, with lovely stonework, and a *cantina* with a vaulted ceiling—and a spring under the floor. Yes, a spring! You lift up a tile with a hook in it and there it is, flowing through a tank a meter deep and a meter wide. And with this vicious heat wave, which has been continuing for the past month and left the countryside parched, there is still a foot of water in it, which seems like a miracle. We would have our own water supply! With a swimming pool to fill on our property down the lane and the high cost of municipal water, this was of great interest to us. Would a hose pipe stretch down the lane, we wondered? Plus it kept the whole house cool in the summer, its own air conditioning. We wondered how it might feel in the winter, would it be really cold and damp? But then realized that we'd only use the house in the summer, so that was not really important.

After we'd signed the papers, we told our neighbors Rosetta and Lina, knowing that word would quickly get around the village. You have to tell them both within a minute of two of the other, though, otherwise they play the game of, Does Rosetta/Lina know? as if they are testing us: which one of them gets told first? We saw Rosetta first so we told her our happy news, and then beetled over to Lina's house to tell her, and the first thing she said was, Does Rosetta know? Yes, we said. Argh, have we upset her? Who knows.

But later that evening, she pulled me aside and told me that Se-

The new dining arbor at the villa

bastiano was pleased—*contento*, in her exact words—that we were buying the house. After 13 years in the village, we are now regarded as family. And we pushed our advantage home: yes, it's so good that house is now in the family! It hasn't gone to strangers! Because the market is so bad and the price so low, Sebastiano was afraid it might have gone to real strangers, not just Italians who had no roots in the village, but to Eastern Europeans, or, even worse, Moroccans. So it was a relief for him to find that we—formerly *stranieri*, but now part of the village—had protected them from an invasion from foreign parts. And it made us happy too. Sebastiano (who is from Sicily, as Lina always whispers when talking about him, as if that explains everything) is very shy and rather sensitive—we are only now shaking hands after 13 years—so I could imagine how uncomfortable he'd be with people he didn't know next door, especially those who spoke a strange language, or even, heaven forbid, had a different skin color. And we wanted him to be happy, too, not upset that we'd bought it out from under him and foiled him in his attempt to add a few parking spaces to his little empire.

. . .

Unfortunately, the woman who was selling the house died of cancer before we could close on the property. It took so long for probate to be sorted out—more than two years—that I lost enthusiasm for it and walked away, losing my 5,000 euro deposit. But in the meantime, while my money had been sitting in the bank waiting for the sale to go through, the dollar had dropped against the euro and I made $5,000 when I changed the money back into dollars! We realized it was just as well as the little house was too small, really, and a few years later we found another larger house that our builder Stefano had bought years before to renovate for his family. But he and his wife had got divorced and apparently he had used the property as a kind of bank, borrowing money against it in the time of easy money and low interest rates, and now it was time to pay the piper. He'd been paying off the mortgage for over 10 years and the price we paid—90,000 euros—just about paid off the balance of the mortgage on his house.

Sebastiano's nightmare came true—the property next to his house was eventually bought by a couple from Poland. They hired our *geometra* Vittorio to make changes, and Sebastiano objected to them—they were in fact a violation of the building code—and he had the work stopped. They soon after got divorced, and we heard recently that the building is up for sale again.

The little house we didn't buy

The Olive Harvest

ONE OF THE INTERESTING THINGS about living in a foreign country is that the year is marked by different traditional events. In the UK, November means the bonfires and fireworks of Guy Fawkes and the solemnity of Armistice Day; in the US it means Thanksgiving and the beginning of the holiday shopping frenzy; in Italy, it means the olive harvest. And so here we are, on a gloriously still autumn day with the foliage all around us turning gold and amber, and a slight mist settling in the valleys and shrouding the distance view of the mountains, preparing to pick olives.

After *porcini* season, after the harvest and all the apples and pears and nuts are gathered and the bean and tomato poles are put away for the winter, olives take over Italian county life. The Italians talk about *le olive* (olives, in the plural, pronounced "ley olivay") as if they were a close family relative, a major event, and a bold-faced name all rolled into one. They worry about their olives constantly, keeping them foremost in their mind. If there is a late April hail storm, they'll shake their heads, saying, "This is not good for the *le olive*;" If the winter is too mild, they'll say, "This is bad for *le olive*." They can't travel or make definite plans in November because of *le olive*, and everyone knows w hat they mean. *Le olive* are part of your life. To neglect one's olives would be sacrilege.

Italians talk about pruning and mowing the grass around the trees as "cleaning" the olives. And olives aren't trees, they are called plants: *piante*. Just as a walnut is *noce*, a nut, an olive tree is a *piante*, a plant. It's very basic nomenclature. I can see the devotion and reverence these country people have for their land and its bounty in our neighbor Maurizio. He has cleaned his olive grove with his parents since he was a little child. And now, at the age of around 60, he comes just about every day from his home in the nearby town of Casola to his mother's house in Reusa to mow and trim and prune, and now, to harvest the olives, just as he has always done. He knows each tree, he prunes each one every year; he witnessed the destruction of the severe frost of 1985, after which there were no olives for ten years until the shoots that had sprung out from roots of the old trees finally bore fruit. His trees are like friends to him. He loves this land that has belonged to his family for generations; he thumps his fist against his heart to show his emotion, this feeling for which there are no words. This is his *paese*, his home, his place in the world. And these are his olives. And I'm beginning to feel the same. There is something mystical about the olive tree and the type of land that grows them. There is something magical about the fruit, which can be purple like large grape, or small and bright green, like a pea. And there is something sensuous about how they feel, silky smooth in the palm of your hand, and when you roll them around a bit, they release a shiny, oily film, and their skin feels like your skin.

It seems to be a point of honor, and a sign of manhood, to collect your own olives. And in Italy, it is a man's job. Each country village becomes a hive of activity at this time of year. Nets are hauled out of the *cantina*, wooden ladders are placed against olive trees, and plastic bottles, terra cotta jars and stainless steel tubs are sterilized ready for the new oil. Our neighbor Angelo has arrived from his suburb of Milan to harvest his few trees, along with his kiwi fruit. Rosetta's oldest son Marcello, who works for a big oil company, has arrived from Milan to become a *contadino* for a week, and his brother Duilio will arrive in a few days to help him. Maurizio, their cousin, has taken the week off work to get his olives harvested, with his mother's help. Now in her mid-80s, she scrambles up and down the olive terraces like a mountain goat, as she has since she married into this family when she was 18. And Pierino arrives to help with ours.

A *contadino* without his own land is not a happy person. Pierino is one such person. But he is happy to work on our land. He does the olives for a portion of the olive oil. We've never found out quite how much; it's just one of those things that, with the local dialect and a stubbornness inherent in Tuscans, we've decided we should just go with the flow, and are grateful for what we get, in terms of both experience and olive oil.

It seems to be a point of pride to harvest every last olive from your trees. Is it because they care what the neighbors think? Kind of like hanging your washing on the line for all to see? Maybe neighbors like to criticize other people's gathering skills—Oh my goodness! they exclaim. They have left olives on their trees! So I beat and comb our olive trees so not a single olive is left. It might seem that one olive doesn't make much of a difference, but you soon realize that in fact each olive does count, as it's only in numbers that you get any olive oil to talk of, it's only a great mass of olives that makes olive oil. So we pick up every last olive off the ground, we slide them off the low-hanging branches with our hands and beat them down with bamboo sticks from the upper branches, or with a little yellow plastic comb attached to a long stick. Once your eye has become accustomed to seeking out the shapes of the olives in the grass, you see them, every one, and you'll find yourself scouring the grass around the olive trees for any escaped olives that can be added to the pile in the barn waiting to be taken to the *frantoio*, the olive mill.

Gathering olives is a delightful occupation, I find. Being out in nature, unrushed, going at the pace, it seems, of the earth's revolution around the sun—what could be better? Nature designed olives to be picked by hand; you can run your hand down a whip-thin bough, a gesture reminiscent of milking a cow, but more like shelling peas. The olives readily come off the bough, but the leaves don't, one of the wonders of nature. I don't like to beat the tree, it seems to go against to the whole idea of the gentle olive tree giving up its fruit to us, wrought from the sun and the rain and the dry earth, the roots of the tree deep down in the clay soil, producing the best form of nourishment that Mother Earth can give us. It all seems like a miracle, considering the barren landscapes where olive trees like to grow.

These days, we hear so much about the health benefits of a Mediterranean diet but I suspect those benefits have as much to do with the harvesting of the olives as the eating of them. It's all those hours spent in the outdoors climbing up and down vertical slopes, scaling ladders, and hauling sacks of olives to the *frantoio*. Plus the olive season lasts quite a while—olives can in fact be ripening all throughout the winter, so it can certainly take weeks, if not months, and sometimes the whole late autumn season and into the winter, if you are fanatical about it, which many people are.

It's when you actually do the olive harvest that all the rituals of cleaning the land and pruning the trees make sense. You clean the grass

Olive trees, Italian style

around the trees so that the land is as smooth as it can be; that way you won't lose olives in long grass, you won't trip on rocks, and you can lay the olive nets flat. The branches are pruned in such a way that they hang down like a fountain so it's easy to slide a hand down the branches to release the olives. On a recent trip to Provence I wondered why the provencal olive trees look so different from the Tuscan variety—they are shorter, stockier, and pruned so brutally that they look more like spiky space aliens with multiple arms than trees, kept low to make the harvesting easier. They seem familiar, though, because of the iconic paintings by Cezanne and Van Gogh. But here in Tuscany, the olive trees are let loose to do their own thing, growing to their natural height of about 15 feet, tangled branches going here and there with loose spires of grey-green foliage wafting gently in the wind like a great sea of olive leaves. I love that part, being able to look out over our valley across a waving field of silver-green, and I am loathe to prune them down too much. But in fact, except for a few trendy youngsters, most of the *contadini* in Tuscany let their olive trees go.

I remember when I planted three mature olive trees in huge terra cotta pots on our terrace at great expense (the pots alone cost more than 100 euros each!) to form a shield from the house that overlooks our terrace, one of our workers, Delio, said, They won't grow well in those pots, you won't get good olives! He couldn't understand that growing olives was not the point; I wanted foliage, a screen of vegetation. Everything for the Italian countryman has to be useful. So the idea of letting my olive trees grow tall and waft prettily in the breeze is not something I can express to Pierino. He has a different idea.

Pierino turns up for work every morning at 8:15 on the dot. It gets light now at about 7 am, so by the time he's got himself up and had a coffee and a brioche and driven here, that's the time it is. He likes to keep a *bella figura*, so arrives in tidy clothes and changes into his working clothes in his battered old blue Fiat, carefully tying a length of twine around his waist and looping it around his thigh to hold an old yellow plastic holster for his most important tool—his clippers. But this day he is armed with a new tool—a chain saw. Suddenly, the vision I have of my grey-green spires waving in the breeze seem doomed. And I am right. Slung over his shoulder he has a safety harness and a stout piece of yellow rope with which to tie his ladder to the tree. He means business. It seems we have finished cleaning the easy trees, the ones at the top of the olive grove, near the old church graveyard where there's a handy stone wall to stand on while we pick olives and prune the unproductive branches; now we have moved to a lower row and it's precarious work. There is at least a ten-foot drop between terraces, which is a long way to fall if you are six feet up a ladder or lose your grip on the tree you are clinging on to. And keeping a foothold on this type of terrain is difficult at the best of times, but when it's draped with slippery plastic *rete* (nets), it's like a luge run. The olives happily run down the nets to the flat terrace below, but so can we, and often do so.

Ron and Pierino gathering olives

Last year's failed olive harvest means that our trees were not pruned, so there's two years work to catch up on. Pierino carefully climbs into his harness, ties his ladder to a tree, hooks himself to a sturdy branch and slowly climbs up, chain saw in hand, ready to saw off the highest branches, the ones that get the most sunlight, and therefore have the most olives. This is a two-fold benefit: we get to pick the olives right off the downed branches and at the same time, the tree gets pruned, or butchered, whichever way you want to look at it. Soon the silence is shattered as the chain saw whirrs its way through stout branches and they come crashing to the ground in a cloud of sawdust and falling olives. It seems like carnage compared to the preceding couple of days. But soon, the whirr of the chain saw stops and the coast is clear for us to gather up the fallen boughs and scoop off the olives, throwing the branches into a pile to be burned later.

Pepe sits patiently at the edge of the terrace, looking over his domain—the valley below where the deer come to eat the last of the season's apples, and who he loves to chase. But there's no one around today, most probably because it's *cinghiale* hunting season and every Wednesday and Sunday droves of men in hunting fatigues and packs of dogs roam through the woods looking for wild boar and scaring the deer away. All of a sudden, the silence is broken by the sound of a helicopter soaring over the mountain and into our valley, hovering dramatically overhead, then taking off and flying over a nearby hill. Looks like the medics, says Pierino, shaking his head. Someone probably fell out of an olive tree. You can't be serious? We ask. Oh yes, he said, looking very serious indeed; it's dangerous work. And especially *dopo pranzo*, we thought, after lunch, with a couple of glasses, or even a bottle, of local wine. It's even more dangerous then.

Soon after, the church bell clanged out its little midday tune and Ron and I set off for our *pranzo di lavoro* at Spino Fiorito, feeling that today we had really earned it. By the time we returned, Pierino had left. Tomorrow is going to be a big day, as we have an appointment at the *frantoio* at 3 pm for the olives to be crushed, so I'm sure he needed to rest up for it. And after a hearty lunch and a glass or two of local wine, we realized it's probably best if we stay away from such dangerous work ourselves.

Yesterday, as we drove into Fivizzano along the country road to do some grocery shopping and were taking a bend just before the village of Teranzano, we nearly ran into an olive bucket sitting in the middle of the road. I'd never spent November in Italy before, so I didn't realize this was the *contadino* equivalent of the reflective red triangle that all vehicles are required to carry. At first, I thought the bucket must have jumped out of someone's truck bed, but as we drove on we saw orange and green nets draped over the road and realized what was happening: an olive grove, whose lower terrace was close to the road, was being cleaned and the bucket was a warning sign to slow down. A couple of elderly men were in the road scooping up the olives and rearranging the nets; maybe one of them had got run over, and that's what the helicopter was looking for. Dangerous work indeed.

At the *frantoio*, a sideline of our local builder's merchant, it was chaos—cars parked everywhere, beaten up Fiat Puntos and Pandas, their back seats stuffed with sacks of olives, and the missus stuffed in the passenger seat with a stainless-steel container on her lap. This was a new *frantoio* with the latest equipment, and they took appointments, so Pierino said it would be quicker to use than the one they used last year, the slow process of crushing the olives with stone wheels. But you'd never know with all the chaos. I peeked inside and saw a large room, more like a warehouse, with shiny new stainless steel equipment running along three sides—a hopper and escalator to take the olives up in the air so the leaves and twigs could be blown off, then a conveyer belt to take them to the washing vats, and then into six grinding tubs, rather like large washing machines, each numbered so six clients' olives could be ground at the same time, then tubes leading into a finer grinder, then thinner tubes leading

Our olives waiting to go through the mill

into the spigot, where people would collect their olive oil. It was a very efficient system, the only thing that seemed organized. But in Italy, often it seems that there is chaos, but in fact everyone instinctively knows what's happening and who's next. And sure enough, we are greeted by an official who checks our name off the list, and then we wait for an hour. Finally, we are allotted a huge plastic tub which holds 250 kilos of olives, and we empty our sacks into the tub. It's a very public affair, and I feel anxious that we might not be able to fill the tub, but happily we do—no shame there!—and I notice that our olives are especially plump and shiny and I'm glad that we did such a good job of culling out the shriveled, the misshapen, and the insect-punctured ones. We wait some more. It was interesting to watch the Italians; they wait patiently—first they'll share the news with each other, talking and gesticulating wildly, getting quite excited as Italians are wont to do. Then they'll have a cigarette and read the newspaper, still an important source of information in Italy. And then they'll start to sing, often one starting with others joining in, then trailing off, and others joining in again. I guess it's kind of like singing in the shower—no one could really hear them against all the noise of the machines. But there's one thing they don't do: they don't snack. You never see Italians eating between meals—no snacks, no chips, no gum being chewed, and certainly no large containers of milky coffee being consumed. They are trained to go for long periods of time between meals. I wish I could do the same, but I am programmed to refuel every four hours or so, so I sneak out to the car where I have stashed a packet of almonds.

Soon, a lanky Ethiopian, an ebony streak of a man with a brilliant smile, at least 6'3" tall, a giant among the crowd of stocky Italians, none of them much taller than me at 5'4", maneuvered a fork-lift truck under our tub and placed it on a large scale. We weighed in at a respectable 178 kilos.

The shiny new equipment was all that we saw of a high-tech world—there was no iPad or computer here, only a pencil, a note pad (the old-fashioned kind, made of paper) and Post-it notes. Our name—Pierino—was scribbled onto a yellow Post-it note, along with 178, and stuck to our tub of olives. Then the tub was maneuvered over to the hopper, along with the yellow note, and we watched as our olives took off up the elevator and through the machinery. The noise was deafening, the smell overwhelming. These machines never stopped, this is the season, everyone needs to have their olives crushed at the same time, and so they work virtually around the clock. As our olives moved through the crushing process, our yellow Post-it note got moved along with it—from the hopper to the crusher to the spigot and then onto our containers, each carefully placed under the tap to make sure not a drop was lost.

We stuck our fingers into the stream of bright green liquid and tasted it; it was sweet and pungent. We filled two containers and weighed them. I wondered why we needed to do that, but it turns out this is the most important part of all. The point about weighing the oil is to see how much we got from our 178 kilos of olives. Apparently that's significant. We got 37 liters, which means that our olives yielded 20 percent of their weight in oil. This meant nothing to us, but Pierino seemed very pleased, as the norm is about 17 percent. The next day we saw Maurizio in the village lane and he said, I heard you got 20 percent! That's great! He had seen Pierino early that morning and he had shared the good news with him. We blushed with pride. Later that day we had lunch at Al Castello in Verrucola with Riccardo and he asked how much oil we'd got, and we told him. That's great, he said. Twenty percent! Terrific! This made me feel even more pleased that I'd thrown out the shriveled olives that would have added to the weight but done nothing to add to the final amount of oil. I was so intoxicated with this praise that I started plotting to buy another olive grove, but after the glow of a fine lunch with Mauro's homemade wine faded, I realized what a foolish idea that was. Who needs more back-breaking work? Certainly not us—we have our hands full.

The next step was to take our Post-it note to the cashier where we'd pay for having the olives crushed. The price was 20 euros per *quintale,* but we were unsure what a *quintale* was. Being used to gallons and pounds, it's easy to get confused when confronted with liters and kilos and *quintales.* Apparently, a *quintale* is one hundred kilos. So for 178 kilos, we were charged the modest sum of 35 euros. The young woman at the cash register was complaining volubly to the man in front of us, saying, What was the point of giving people appointments when they never turned up on time? Some turned up early, some late, and some arrived with twice as many olives as they said they'd bring! I sympathized with her; it was already 6 pm, pitch dark, and there was still a throng of cars filled with olives crowding the parking lot. We maneuvered our Jeep out through the waiting cars and headed for home, taking half the olive oil, with Pierino getting the other half. We still can't figure out why, when we own the olive grove and did half the work, we only get half the oil, but then, we can't quite figure out why Pierino comes every year at this time to pick the olives. He never arrives at any other time to "clean"—to mow and prune—we do all that. But he doesn't speak English and we don't speak much Italian, at least, not his kind, mostly dialect, and anyway he's getting old and set in his ways, so we stick to the arrangement. So we both went home with about 18 litres of the freshest, most luscious olive oil you could imagine.

To celebrate, we brought some fresh crusty bread and a bottle of Prosecco and toasted our new oil. But we are only halfway done—there's at least another 178 kilos to go, maybe more.

Pierino tasting the new olive oil

Chaos in Tuscany

ALL OVER TUSCANY, and maybe all over Italy, people are in a panic. Italians are conservative by nature, and they don't like change. But the times they are a-changing and Italy is becoming eco-aware, so our familiar way of disposing of rubbish is changing.

For decades a familiar sight in Italy, part of the landscape in fact, has been the large green communal trash bins distributed about every half mile along the country roads, and in every town and village center, there is a cluster of different colored bins for recycling glass, paper and plastic. But now in an heroic attempt to cut down on the amount of trash that is thrown away, we are being asked to separate out just about everything that can be recycled, except for certain items that qualify as trash and are listed item by item: old toothbrushes, pens and paint brushes, floppy disks, disposable razors, old makeup—the list goes on for twelve lines of items, some of which I've never heard of.

But the good news is that now we can recycle tin cans, which I always felt really bad about throwing away in the trash, and every single bit of plastic, including blister wraps and plastic bags, which is thrilling. This means that our bag of *resto secco indifferenziato*, or plain trash, amounts to almost nothing, with our piles of paper, plastic and glass growing by the day, but happily all recyclable. *Umido* all goes into the compost pile; the *comune* is bringing us a fancy composter for the garden, but first they have to come and inspect the garden to make sure we make the grade. We are still waiting. Meanwhile, we've dug a hole in a corner of the olive grove where for now we pile the *umido*.

That's the easy part; the difficult part is that we now have individual bins in bright colors—red, green, blue, brown and white—for the different types of trash. And moreover, the red bin, the actual trash, is locked with a special card with a chip, so that only we can open it. This is high tech stuff, and as such, has completely confused all the elderly people who live up in these mountain villages. They are wandering around, bewildered. The word *bidone*, which I've never heard before, is on everyone's lips. It means dustbin. And instead of wandering along to the trash containers whenever we want, we now have to put out our gaily colored bins on special days. We have each been provided with a complicated calendar printed in full color so we know when that will be: *vetro/lattine* (glass/metal) every Friday, *umido* (or *organico*) every Tuesday and Thursday, *indifferenziato* every Thursday, and *carta* (paper) on Tuesdays, but only twice a month, with *plastico* on alternating Thursdays, and an *eco-mobile*, a van, comes by once a month to pick up any stuff that won't fit into those little bins. Got that? Good. We are still struggling.

This was all apparently to be a plan for the future. We'd been given the bins and the calender, but our old communal bins were still there, taking up most of the space in our tiny village parking lot, so we all kept on using them. Then the day of reckoning arrived: one morning a large truck came by with a crane and hauled all the bins into the truck bed and drove them off to the graveyard for discontinued trash containers. And then we realized we were all alone; we had to get to grips with the new system. So we carefully sorted out all our trash as we used it and triumphantly carried our bins out to the road on the morning of the first Friday after the large bins were removed. We ran into Miralda who told us we were too late, the truck had come by at 6 am. Better luck next time! Frustrated, we returned up the lane to our house and marked our calenders to make sure we didn't forget the next week.

At lunch that day, we discussed the issue with Riccardo and asked if his town, Monzone, has the same problem. Yes, he said, but we've got used to it by now. But we missed this week, we complained, and now we'll have to put out two bags next week, and our bins only fit one bag! Don't worry, he said, just put it by the side of the road. But is that allowed under the new rules, we asked? Who cares about the new rules? he answered. Andrea picks up the trash, and he'll pick up whatever you put out. And who is Andrea, we asked? Miralda's son, he said, he lives in Monzone and picks up the trash for the whole area. So that's how Miralda knew what to do and how; her son was the trash pickup guy. Suddenly we felt better. It was all in the family; we wouldn't be fined and shamed.

Each container for general rubbish has a personal microchip for each householder so no one else can use that bidone. And your trash bags also have a micro chip! There's no escaping the *eco-vigili*—big brother is watching you. Maurizio said that one hapless person who hadn't quite got the hang of it tossed his neatly bundled bag of trash into the local river, as the Italians had been doing for centuries—but it had his personal bar code on it! He was caught and fined 600 euros. A warning to us all! It makes me feel fortunate that we don't have raccoons in Italy.

. . .

GUEST COMMENT:

We have loved every minute of our week in Italian paradise.

— Annabel, Will, Rich and Cat, London

Il Vecchio Mulino

The Old Mill in Casette

WE BOUGHT THE HOUSE in Casette from Stefano in 2018 so that Ron could have a place to stay in the summers when the villa was rented out, as well as another project for him to work on. It was such a cute old stone building with a stream running alongside it—I quite fell in love with it when I first saw it and felt a twinge of envy that it wasn't mine. The house had been a water mill, about 500 years old; it had never been renovated and had no water connection, no electric-

The old mill in Casette with the stream on the left

Riccardo working on the Old Mill in Casette

ity, no septic system, no windows, and two beaten-up wood panels for a front door with a padlock on it to keep people out—but not the bats, the top floor was full of them. It had a very bad layout; there were three rooms on each floor—there were three floors—and the connecting doors were on the extreme left as you went from room to room, making the rooms very dark. And there was a hideous iron staircase right in the middle of the living room as you entered; it was only after I realized that by moving the staircase to the middle room and opening up the living room to the kitchen, basically opening up the house by moving the doors to the middle of the house rather than the extreme left, that the house would "work." We found a new carpenter who lives in Gragnola—the town that the village of Casette is a part of—and he did a great job of making the windows and doors for the house. And then we asked him if he could make the staircase; it would be a tricky job because none of the walls was square and the space was tight. But he said yes, he thought he could do it. I held my breath while he made it; if it couldn't fit in the space, all the work we'd done on the house so far would be for nothing. When it was finished, he brought it in piece by piece and assembled it in the house, bolting it to the stone walls and installing each wooden step individually. And it turned out to be magnificent—made of oak, it was light and airy and perfect for the space; in fact, it was better than I had imagined.

As of this writing, the renovations are almost complete—we just have to add a balcony, renovate the front steps, and build a wall to make a courtyard garden; then it will be done. And then I will have another garden to design!

The back of the house and future courtyard garden

What the Bells Tell Us

February 7th, 2021

THIS MORNING, just after the church bell had struck nine, I heard the bell toll. I knew immediately it was for Lina. She had finally gone, in her 90th year, gone to the place where her beloved husband, son, sister and two brothers had gone before her, some so many years ago, and who she had mourned since their passing.

We can't feel sorry for Lina, though we all loved her and we'll miss her terribly, but we all knew how much she was suffering. So instead we feel gladness that her suffering is over and she is in the hands of God. We think of her often, even though she recently moved to the neighboring village of Casola to live with her son Maurizio and his family, and we are filled with gratitude that she was the welcoming and loving soul that we were so lucky to have as our neighbor when we first arrived in Reusa.

We bought this old house in 2003, and met Lina and her husband Roberto one fine April day just before we were to pass papers and become the proud owners of this dilapidated ruin. We had gone to Italy for a week to buy the house, and drove to the house before we actually owned it, as the closing was held up by a week. We started by clearing the weeds from the stone courtyard in front of the building, so excited to be embarking upon a new adventure. Lina and Roberto were so helpful and friendly, telling us where we could dump the weeds and rubbish, and inviting us in to see their house and share a simple lunch with them. The first thing we saw as we entered their courtyard was a tiny America flag; it turned out that Roberto had been born in the USA when his father had gone there in the early

Gillian and Lina in the courtyard of her magnificent old house

part of the 20th century to find work. He had returned during the depression and Roberto, being the youngest of the four sons, had returned to Italy with him. He soon met Lina, a strikingly-beautiful dark-haired teenager who lived in the neighboring village of Groppolo, and they married. Lina moved from her parents' house up the hill into the grand house next door to ours.

Lina told me she was born in 1923, in a small stone-built terraced house in Groppolo, one part of the five hamlets of the village of Reusa. Her father, Lino Tesconi, was from Fiasciano (Maliano), near Fivizzano, and her mother, Elsa Bondi, was born in Reusa. The couple had four children—Amadeo, Lina, Luciano, and Lilliana.

They went to the school in Groppolo, which was in the house that later become the home of Lina's sister Lilliana and her husband Mario, and since their passing, now belongs to Mario and Lilliana's

Lina and her son Maurizio crushing grapes and feeding the juice into their cantina

daughter Nicoletta and her husband Piero (they will be our neighbors at our "new" house in Groppolo.) The school was in the front room. School started at age 7 and were there for five years, until 11 or 12 years of age. Kids would come from as far away as Padula to go to the school. After that, they'd work in the fields with their parents, looking after sheep, helping to collect and chop wood, and gathering chestnuts in the autumn. Lina told me there were lots of illegitimate children in the village at that time, which is why the school was always full of children!

When she was young, after school and before she was married, Lina worked in the home and helped to take care of her brother Luciano, who was mentally handicapped. When her other brother Amadeo was 22 or 23, he left for Corsica to find work, and then went on to Belgium to work in the coal mines. There he met Rosetta, who, when the couple returned, became Lina's closest friend and neighbor. Rosetta, at 90+, is still with us, making her rounds every day, checking on everyone in the village and carrying the gossip from one family to another.

Lina was eleven when war broke out; she said life didn't change much because they were self-sufficient, they had their chickens, rabbits, sheep, cows, olives and chestnuts. One day towards the end of the war, the Americans arrived in Castelnuovo and the Germans were in Fivizzzano and they had raging battles, with bombs flying overhead. The villagers took refuge during air raids in shelters the men had dug on the road up to Groppolo, you can still see remnants of them by the side of the road, on the left. They didn't shelter in the wine cellars in case a bomb hit their house. There were escaped prisoners of war in those days hiding out in remote sheds and barns up in the mountains. They survived pretty well in the summer, but in the winter their tracks were harder to hide and they were more often than not

Lina and her nephew Freddie who lives in America

recaptured. The men of the Resistance were always blowing up roads and bridges, said Lina, though it didn't do much good, as it meant the locals couldn't get to the next village. And it angered the Germans, who sought devastating reprisals, murdering the entire populations of remote villages, women and children included, in Vinca, Regnano Alto and Mommio. These atrocities are still commemorated every year in this region on Liberation Day in April.

The first time I met Lina, in 2003, when she was in her early 70s and Roberto her husband was still alive, she seemed such a vibrant personality. I remember her sitting on the back of the trailer of their old tractor, her feet in rubber boots, swinging her legs like a teenager as her husband drove up the mountain to collect firewood. That is a happy woman, I remember thinking. Sadly, her happiness was not to last, because within a year both Roberto and her younger sister Lilliana had passed away within a week of each other, both of cancer. Lina was devastated. She drew comfort from the love and support of her two sons, Doriano, who lived in La Spezia, and Maurizio, who lives nearby in Casola.

Lina lived in Reusa for her entire life; she never learned to drive and in her later years, rarely left the village, though when she was younger she made many trips to New Jersey, where her husband's relatives lived. She felt that she was living in Paradise, and there was no reason to go anywhere else.

Her son Maurizio would come to our village every day to visit Lina and tend the land that had been in his family for so many generations—olive groves, wood lots, and vineyards. They had sold some land to us, which meant that our olive grove and meadow are contiguous with theirs, so we were always interacting and helping each other out, and still are. I would look forward to visiting Lina at her beautiful ancient house, remaining just as it had always been since it was built, untouched by modern hands; I loved sitting by the fire with her, listening to her tell tales of the village and its residents, all members of one large family, and how they lived off the land, as their ancestors had for hundreds of years before; how they harvested chestnuts in the autumn to make chestnut flour for bread and cakes, and take the milking cows up to the mountain pasture in the spring, and slaughter the pig each year before winter set in. She told me that most people kept chickens and rabbits for the pot, and there was plenty of deer and wild boar around for those who had guns. Her brother Amadeo owned the hillside that rises up behind his house, all the way up to Groppolo, and its rich soil provided enough vegetables for the entire village. They survived the cold and damp of the winters by gathering in the *essiccatoio*, the chestnut-drying-house, a small barn with a rack for drying the chestnuts that sat six feet above an open fire in the middle of the barn. Benches lined the interior of the *essiccatoio* where the local inhabitants would sit and chat and shelter from the chill and damp of the winter. In the summer, they sat around a stone bench in the village's tiny piazza, playing music and catching up on the gossip.

Lina was patient and kind, and helped me to learn Italian by talking slowly and distinctly, unlike some other Italians who tend to talk at the speed of a machine gun. She was able to speak Italian, not dialect; she was very proud that she had learned to speak real Italian at school, as many locals speak only dialect, having never learned proper grammar (and oh, those verbs! I have sympathy for them). Every time I visited, she would give me something to take home—eggs from her chickens, tomatoes and herbs from her garden, bottles of jam and preserves, a pot of salsa—I never came back empty handed. In return I'd bring her geraniums and seedlings of basil and parsley from the market in the spring, as she did not drive and seldom got out much to do any shopping. Instead, after the village shop closed, vans selling food started to come to the village. She loved nature, and she was invariably to be found in her garden in fine weather, tending her *orto* or raking hay in the vineyard and olive grove.

Neighbors Miralda and Carla preparing the church for mass

The church was the focal point of village life, even though all the villagers seemed to have different points of view when it came to religion, dismissing the Pope as superfluous, or worse, and revering the Virgin Mary, the "mother goddess," to the point that the crucifix was barely noticeable in the church. For Lina, being so close to Nature, Mother Mary was everything.

The inside of the little church of Reusa has a distinct feminine quality, the surfaces covered in white lace, the walls decorated with images of cherubs and angels and a tranquil virgin gazing at a blue sky. It's definitely a woman's place, and often, when the men feel they are obliged to attend a service, usually weddings and funerals, they will hang about outside, shifting from foot to foot, until the ordeal is over. Lina went to mass every week with Rosetta and the other ladies of the village. The village priest has to take care of so many village churches that our designated day for mass was Saturday, and that has recently been changed to Tuesday. But now that so many of the year-round residents have passed on, it seems that soon the church may not have a weekly service at all.

Lina was a peacemaker; her philosophy to living in the village was to get on with everyone, and to argue with no one. And there are some strange personalities in this village! Everyone loved Lina, she was *bravissima*—kind, generous, friendly, intelligent, and patient. How much we will miss her. And with her goes the memory of the kind of life that was lived in this village for centuries; not only have we lost Lina but we have lost the living memory of those times.

Easter lunch at Lina's house with the family, Maurizio and his wife Maura on the far left and Gillian on the far right

All Good Things Must Come to an End . . .

WHEN LINA DIED and her son Maurizio sold her house to an English woman who modernized it beyond recognition, we felt the soul had gone out of the village. Plus we were both in our 70s and tired of running a rental villa, as wonderful and appreciative, for the most part, as our guests were. So we decided to list it for sale. Soon after we got an offer and sold it 20 years to the day from when we first saw it, at the end of September, to a couple from Milan who wanted it as a year-round home. They fell in love with it at first sight; it was just what they were looking for. They gave us until the end of October to move all our things out. But we had help—a couple from the US, Kristy and Adam, and their teenage son, who stayed with us for a month, and our friend John from the UK, who had visited the villa every year since we first bought it and had worked ceaselessly cutting grass and fixing lawn mowers and painting walls—he is a real Mr. Fixit. It was the best of times and the worst of times; the best because the villa was full of people and we enjoyed a communal dinner together every night, taking turns to cook; the worst because we were moving out, and our lives seemed unimaginable without Casa della Quercia in it; our hearts were quite bruised. But we gritted our teeth and started to move our stuff out, starting with the linen closets in the barn, which held enough sheets and blankets and bedspreads for 12 beds. Fortunately, our neighbor Ensina offered us her garage to store our things temporarily; it is right next to the villa so we didn't have to move them far. We tied the wardrobes to a wheel barrow and just wheeled them over. All the metal outdoor furniture went into Marcello's (Amadeo's son) cantina, some of our stuff went to Patrizia's garage, and the rest went into storage until we could find somewhere permanent to put it all.

Kristy, Coleman and Adam Prince who spent a month with us during their year of traveling around the world to help us move our belongings out of the villa

We had already furnished the house in Casette, but we had so much more furniture—we were bulging at the seams! We decided we should buy another smaller house somewhere—preferably in the *comune* of Casola, if not in the same village, as we still had many friends there. Plus my Italian residency card is from Casola and I didn't want to change it. Our house in Casette is in the *comune* of Fivizzano and the one time I went to the town hall to ask a question they seemed very hostile.

There are two ways you can buy and sell property in Italy: you can go to a top-drawer realtor such as Sotheby's, or in our area L'Architrave, who charge a hefty premium, five percent from the seller plus five percent from the buyer, or you can go into a bar on a Friday night and ask, Does anyone know of a house that we can buy? Italians hate to pay a big commission to sell their property—they would rather let it languish on the market for years than pay five percent to sell it. So

View of the town of Casola from the river

we went into the bar in Casola on a Friday night and asked around. Maurizio was there, and his wife too—oddly sitting at a different table with a bunch of women friends. Soon the whole place was buzzing and Maurizio fielded the suggestions.

It transpired that a distant relative of his had a house for sale in the *antico borgo* of Casola, almost next door to the bar; it had been in the family for generations but had been badly damaged in the earthquake of 2013. It was an old house, as ancient as the town itself—in fact, it was part of the wall that formed a kind of fortress at the edge of the river, six stories in all. It was in a way a vertical farm, with the top two floors serving as living quarters and a stone-flagged terrace overlooking the river below—be still my heart!—and another four floors descending down, like a windowless dungeon, with rabbit hutches, chicken coops, olive oil vats carved out of stone, and a cantina. And, right at the bottom, a cow shed that had access to a patch of green grass at the river's edge. The price was low and we realized why when we saw the carnage as we were about to descend into the lower levels—the earthquake had jumbled up the massive stones of the staircase as if they were children's wooden building blocks. It was ruined, this lovely ancient building. It was a sad sight. What a trage-dy! I don't think anyone would be willing or wise to invest the money to repair the damage.

Then he said, My great aunt has a house for sale up in Groppolo—which is part of the village of Reusa. That's great, we said, let's go take a look. So the next day, we climbed the ancient footpath that leads up to the village to inspect the house. One part was a stone house, many centuries old, perhaps five, and had an imposing stone portico with a patio on top with a panoramic view of the mountains. The other part was a "new" house attached that his great aunt had built back in the 1940s. We had walked past it countless times during our time in Reusa, but hadn't realized its potential because of two large ever-green trees that obscured the view. But they had recently been cut down and revealed the magnificent view. We were sold. And it spoke

Ron inspecting the "new" house in Groppolo

to us, saying those immortal words: Save me, love me, fix me up! But best of all, it's "in the family"—Lina's sister Lilliana and her husband Mario had lived next door and now that they have both passed on, their daughter Nicoletta and her husband Piero currently live there—in fact, they share the stone courtyard behind the house with us.

We signed the purchase agreement on my last day in Italy in May of 2022, sending the deposit by wire the next week. Maurizio's great-aunt Divina was at this time 102 years old and she was selling it with her four grandchildren. Unfortunately, one of the grandchildren died suddenly (we had thought that Divina herself was the one who was going to go!) so things got held up in probate; then the geometra went on a camping trip to Morocco for a few months to escape the dreary winter months, so when we arrived in Italy the following March not much progress had been made. But in Italy, we have learned, there are long periods when nothing happens, then all of a sudden it's all systems go. And so it was with this process with a last minute rush to get all the documents in order and a year after we had first signed the purchase and sale document, we were ready to close the deal.

At the closing, which took three hours, there were ten of us in the notiao's office, which by chance happened to be the very same notiao who had been involved when we bought Roberto's barn. He didn't recognize me, but I recognized him. He looked a lot older and was a little shaky and he only got through the long process with the help of his daughter. Evidently he is a friend of the family—Divina and her grandchildren chatted away with him during the intervals when a page of the contract had to be printed out again when someone made a mistake with their signature—and they wouldn't dream of using anyone else. But when the ordeal was over, we owned the house! Finally! We had to pinch ourselves, it seemed unreal. We immediately drove up to Groppolo and cleaned out the rubbish that the family had left (fortunately we had stipulated in the purchase and sale agreement that the house had to be empty of furniture—but we forgot to say empty of rubbish!)—and we dug up a flower bed that was full of weeds and planted a row of lavender to make it our own.

An amusing thing happened six months after we had sold the villa; we were in the house in Casette one evening in April, about to settle in for the night, when there was tentative knock on the door. A man stood there—we weren't sure who he was though we vaguely recognized him, but we invited him in. He said something about *falegname* (carpenter) so we thought he had come to admire the beautiful staircase that our new carpenter had made for us, which made the whole layout of the new house "work." He duly admired it,

The courtyard of the house in Groppolo that we share with neighbors Nicoletta and Piero

but then said something in Italian about us owing money—he spoke no English—and it dawned on us that it was Mario's son Alberto come to extract the final payment for the work he had done at Casa della Quercia! Mario had heard through the grapevine that we had sold the villa and wanted to settle up with us. We held our breath as he told us how much we owed him—was it *cinque cento* or *cinque mila*?—and breathed a huge sigh of relief when he said *cinque cento*. So we gladly wrote a check for 500 euros and shook hands with him. We asked how Mario was; he told us he'd continued to work until he was 85 but had now retired. We wonder what had happened to his huge store of seasoned chestnut wood, since Alberto had not inherited his father's skill for woodworking, nor for running a restaurant, evidently.

So now we have embarked on renovating the house in Groppolo and realize that we have a summer house and a winter house; how lucky we are! The house in Casette is more convenient, being 20 minutes closer to the city of Aulla and the coast, while the house in Groppolo is immersed in the most beautiful countryside and surrounded by people we love. And so the adventure continues.

Made in the USA
Coppell, TX
31 December 2023

27070123R00105